Trust

Trust

Releasing the Energy to Succeed

Rita Cruise O'Brien

JOHN WILEY & SONS, LTD
Chichester · New York · Weinheim · Brisbane · Singapore · Toronto

Other Wiley Editorial Offices

John Wiley & Sons, Inc., 605 Third Avenue,
New York, NY 10158-0012, USA

Wiley-VCH Verlag GmbH, Pappelallee 3,
D-69469 Weinheim, Germany

John Wiley & Sons Australia Ltd, 33 Park Road, Milton,
Queensland 4064, Australia

John Wiley & Sons (Asia) Pte Ltd, 2 Clementi Loop #02-01,
Jin Xing Distripark, Singapore 129809

John Wiley & Sons (Canada) Ltd, 22 Worcester Road,
Rexdale, Ontario M9W 1L1, Canada

A catalogue record for this book is available from the British Library

ISBN 0-471-49130-6

Typeset in 12/15pt Garamond by Footnote Graphics, Warminster, Wiltshire
Printed and bound in Great Britain by Biddles Ltd, Guildford and King's Lynn
This book is printed on acid-free paper responsibly manufactured from sustainable forestry,
in which at least two trees are planted for each one used for paper production.

*To the people at British Telecom
who first convinced me
that people had a great deal more
to offer at work*

and

*to Sarah for her
most astute
reflections on work,
motivation and trust*

Contents

Preface

I first became aware of 'how much more people had to offer' (hence the dedication of *Trust*) when I was working with British Telecom in the early 1990s, prior to the research on this book. I was struck in meetings and focus groups on the development of employee commitment to quality, that people had much more to give than they were willing to offer. They regarded the BT of those days as a very low trust organization whose management rated very poor results on annual employee satisfaction surveys. Management paid lip service to the improvement of service quality, but at this time were primarily driven by other priorities. As one person commented, 'We had customer service before they reinvented it with capital letters!'

The idea for this book came to me in the mid-1990s at the height of interest in promoting total quality management in the USA and Europe. At that time Japanese firms, which had taken on the ideas of the American quality guru, W. Edward Deming, decades earlier, were the model of quality performance worldwide. The tide has turned now with some European and American firms outperforming Japanese firms, notably in car manufacturing. The overall impact of quality efforts in the 1990s in Europe and North America was varied. A minority of firms felt that quality had a lasting impact on its competitiveness. Part of the reason was the confusion of ends and means, allowing quality bureaucracies to swell, notably in the case of Florida Power and Light, which won the coveted Deming Prize in 1989, but whose CEO admitted that the whole exercise had little or no impact on productivity. Most firms simply did not implement the activities in full, while others concentrated on the mechanics to the frustration of employees.[1]

The research for this book was carried out while I was Reseach Fellow at the London Business School from 1992 to 1995, working with Professor Chris Voss in Operations Management. The research was supported very generously by the Gatsby Charitable Foundation and the Science and Engineering Research Council. I am grateful to Lord Sainsbury for his early support of this project which demonstrated his keen interest in research to improve performance in British industry – a role he now ably fulfils in government. Chris Voss was a splendid guide to quality issues and published widely in the field himself. He and colleagues in the Organizational Behaviour Group at the School were a great source of encouragement of my work on what it takes to get front-line employees committed to new targets of high performance based on quality. I am indebted to Mark Fenton O'Creevy, now at the Open University, who helped design the questionnaire returned by 1000 employees in the six firms in which I worked, and was of immeasurable help in interpreting the results. Mary Campbell, the Editor of *Business Strategy Review,* gave very helpful comments on a draft of the manuscript. Diane Taylor at Wiley believed in the project from the outset and waited patiently for delivery. Jamie Latham developed the splendid idea for the cover. I was fortunate to have been named a Scholar in Residence at the Bellagio Study Center by the Rockefeller Foundation in 1994 when I was grappling with the theoretical and conceptual aspects of trust in the economic and other social science literature. My husband Donal, who was working on his own book, accompanied me to Italy where we made lasting friends among fellow scholars. His support and encouragement have always been a source of inspiration.

SEARCHING FOR ANSWERS IN PERFORMANCE IMPROVEMENT

I have asked, listened, analysed and lectured about trust for more than five years. My personal quest began one evening on a small village hotel outside Stoke-on-Trent. Busy on my laptop, I was transcribing notes from a quality team meeting at an ICL plant (which became the independent Design to Distribution – D2D in 1994). I had been looking for what made employees want to achieve higher performance targets in order to secure a new contract with Sun Microsystems, vital to the survival of the plant and its workforce. I was persuaded that employee commitment was required – people giving of their hearts and minds to the new performance campaign – wrenching themselves out of traditional manufacturing practices in order to enter the world of fierce global competition. I was looking for an explanation – academics would call it an 'intervening variable' – that indicated how to turn employee involvement into commitment. I felt it would have to be trust. My effort to try to understand its potential power had a considerable effect.

Throughout the following two years, working with five other firms, I was able to learn of the power and potential of trust as I observed the low energy in low trust firms. I saw trust destroyed with catastrophic consequences, for the people involved and for the enterprise. I became aware of the very painful process of trying to rebuild it. My education in these matters was taking place in the aftermath of downsizing and restructuring in British manufacturing firms on both sides of the Atlantic.

The evidence contained in this book is based on research in six British firms from 1993 to 1995. Apart from ICL Manufacturing/D2D, they are called by names which I have given them. The research first considered the efforts to generate broad-based employee participation in the improvement of competitive performance, by looking at the employee-involvement programmes developed as part of total quality management. This research was based on the assumption that employee commitment was required in order to achieve high rates of conformance to standards, keep fault rates low, and maintain high performance over time. The method of research was both qualitative and quantitative, including months of direct observation and interviews in each of the firms, the presentation of detailed case studies to each of the collaborating organizations, and culminating in a questionnaire survey of more than 1000 'front-line' employees in these firms.

Reflecting on the intensive qualitative fieldwork once completed, trust appeared to be an essential variable to explain the potential for changing relationships within the firm in a wide variety of individual or group situations. High- and low trust relationships and organizations were examined on the basis of identical criteria. This helped to identify a broader set of explanatory factors, with potentially wider significance for the firm than simply performance improvement.

It became obvious during many hours of observing teams working on process improvement that I was looking at the gradual, halting, often faltering, development of mutual confidence between front-line managers and their teams, among different cross-functional groups and mutually dependent line teams. The new foundation of the relationship, based on a collaborative contribution of information and knowledge to the process, seemed to create a potential opportunity for better working relationships, whatever else was happening more generally in the organization. This process was of central importance to the success or non-success of employee involvement in process improvement. Success was far less dependent on the design or implementation of programmatic change than on the atmosphere of the local work environment, its climate and culture.

In my sample employee commitment to the firm, division or site appeared to be less important than local work relationships. The destruction of the traditional social contract based on job security in most of the collaborating firms had not been replaced with a new contract. Participating in process improvement did not constitute a lead into a new form of contract. Programmes such as quality management were trying to set a new agenda for work by promoting novel forms of collaboration between employees and management, attempting to create a mutual interest in improved competitive performance. Even in firms with successful quality programmes and relatively progressive human resource policies, employee commitment to the organization seemed to depend on the organization of work locally and the relationships which sustained it. Process improvement was best focused on the activities of front-line employees in manufacturing, or customer-facing employees in services.

Shopfloor employees in the survey seemed willing, even keen, to contribute to process improvement initially as a matter of pride, and their self-perception as 'quality employees'. Our survey findings discussed in Chapter 3 demonstrate a high level of job involvement. Valuable assets of job pride and involvement were not necessarily captured in the efforts of new performance teams. While employees had sufficient information about the new goals for performance improvement, and while they understood its significance to competitive performance, low trust in almost all the firms affected their willingness to give as much as they might have either by contributing their knowledge or committing themselves to improved performance. Thus the intrinsic value of job pride and high job involvement remained outside these new processes – untapped because of an atmosphere of low trust.

TRUST: SOME QUESTIONS ANSWERED

When I introduce trust to business audiences, I am immediately confronted with sceptics. The questions they have asked are customarily about loyalty, security, pay and participation A new one has been added: the effect of increased use of e-mail and homeworking on trust customarily based on traditional face-to-face interaction. Employee loyalty is usually linked to customer loyalty. But I shall argue that loyalty is not enough in the current competitive environment. Loyalty is not a dynamic concept like trust. And it is not certain that the most loyal people in an organization really provide the best customer service. To be loyal to an institution or organization – rare though it is these days – adds some value, but lacks depth, significance, and resilience for the competitive demands of the new economy.

Security

How can you even consider trust in today's workplace?
There is no longer any security; how can there be trust?

The decline and disappearance of the traditional social contract based on job security had an inevitable impact on trust. This is particularly so when there is little new strategic orientation or new set of values which are widely accepted throughout the firm. Trust, however, is not based on security alone. It is possible to radically restructure and reorient a firm and maintain trust, and conversely to lose the trust or people in a situation of apparent job security.

The ICL Manufacturing plant at Ashton, near Manchester, was constantly under threat, and required managers to pay continuous attention to structure, process and performance criteria. Yet its people were continuously informed of what they had to do to respond to the external competitive threat by the site management and other members of the management team, who were almost fully occupied in the search for new business. Trust did not falter, once created, despite the uncertainty of the future and high demands on employees.

Milliken Industries is a celebrated multinational which won many awards for its people-centred management in a low-skill environment. In its contract carpet factory in Lancashire, the story was different. Although management had every intention of maintaining jobs throughout the recession of the early 1990s, morale and trust were at a very low ebb because site management found little time to inform people on a regular basis of the efforts to bring work and new customers to the firm. Job losses in the factories around them did not reassure their people. At ICL, continuous information mitigated deep anxiety, while at Millikin, its absence created unwarranted fear.

Pay

Why not simply pay people to support increased performance improvement?

The current efforts to improve staff retention are principally aimed at high flyers with specialist skills or expertise. But what about the rest of the firm? Involving people in performance improvement may be generated by incentives based on job redesign, flexibility and performance results, all of which have value. Incentive schemes based on reward for front-line people are more complex. Performance-related pay schemes can become arcane, with little actual financial reward distributed to individuals below senior management. Incentive schemes intended to generate improved performance can also militate against involvement by stressing only the contractual nature of the relationship. Introducing such schemes in an environment will not necessarily generate trust.

The second major question which is regularly asked is why not just pay employees a bonus, or provide an incentive scheme? Years of analysis have not conclusively proven that this is the best way to improve performance on a long-term basis.[2] Performance-related pay, in particular, relies on the mistaken view that what motivates people is primarily reward. Some believe that such schemes at best buy short-term compliance, but fail to make an impact on attitude or commitment to task over a period of time.[3] The motivation such schemes may generate somehow runs out; the schemes – usually very complicated – become ossified or are manipulated. Such schemes are also notorious for record faking.

We know that more than just incentive pay is needed to promote innovation in the firm or to introduce employee ideas on a continuous basis. Few breakthroughs in competitive performance or diffused innovation seem to be grounded in pay and performance schemes alone. Reward schemes can even destroy cooperation and have been known to discourage people from being imaginative or taking risks.

Participation

Isn't it sufficient to get people involved in performance improvement?
Why bother about trust?

Getting people involved in performance-improvement schemes was very popular in the 1990s. Most of these efforts have yielded little lasting impact on people's motivation or their individual performance. In many instances, such efforts were largely programmatic interventions 'bolted on' to the customary activities of the firm, which failed to take root, change fundamentally the way things were done or make any lasting impact.

Employee-involvement schemes usually began with training programmes on the new aims and objectives of quality, just-in-time management or customer service improvement schemes. People were often called off-site to sessions with other employees at different levels and different parts of the firm. Once back on the job, local leadership often faltered, and initiatives seemed inconsistent. People generally did not 'buy in' over a long period of time, however enthusiastic they may have been at the beginning.

Participation, as we shall see in Chapters 1 and 2, is generated on the basis of new aims, ideas and programmes which often fail because of lack of tenacity or consistency in management initiatives. Consistency is one of the key qualities management requires to sustain trust. It often appears to be in short supply. Participation peters out because people are not provided with accurate and frequent information on how they are doing, in a form which they can understand. This information is a vital ingredient to helping people understand where they are in the process and how they are doing currently.

Participation, or the willingness to participate fully, often becomes a missed opportunity, as people are not recognized or rewarded for the improvement they have achieved. To participate may be to give of oneself rather little, or to join in with something because it has been prescribed by the organization. Between that and trust lies a missed opportunity to respond to something for which people are looking – an opportunity to be more fulfilled at work and to be more appreciated for the effort made.

E-networks

People are increasingly using email to communicate in most firms. Does the absence of face-to-face contact have an impact on trust in an organization?

The effectiveness of technology depends not only on the design and efficiency of networks but also on the value of communication and richness of personal networks that sustain their life. Technology is only as effective as the people who create the value are able to communicate it. In a corporate world increasingly dependent on electronic communication and electronic business networks, the trust that can be created by the written or spoken word can be just as effective as face-to-face communication

Instead of 'walking the job', executives who have learned the gift of effective e-mail contact and communication can build new forms of trust in a fraction of the time. Many employees feel that they can e-mail the chief executive, while they would not dream of knocking on his door or stopping him in the corridor. This breaks down the communication barriers between top people and employees: it reduces the significance of the funnel of information through middle management.

'E-business' networks have the advantage that people can select the time when they wish to communicate, and may give an opportunity to people who are more reserved or shy to become a vigorous part of a networked relationship or group. The distance between people is nullified and communication can be relaxed. These do not necessarily attenuate trust relations or devalue trust in any way. They add a potential extra dimension to the scope and impact of trust.

It could be argued – somewhat counter-intuitively – that the increased use of e-mail can influence trust positively, but it will not create trust where there is none. It will not create trust in and of itself. But where collaboration is strong, the ease of e-mail can enhance rather than detract from it.

Some chief executives and senior managers have used corporate e-mail effectively – to introduce themselves and communicate openly with employees on a regular basis. They use e-mail to enhance the frequency and ease of communication. All depends on the quality of the content, the tone of the message and the context into which it fits. Some people in an organization – who may not shine in meetings – may be able to get their points across to senior management more easily.

In an international company, people can sustain a dialogue much more easily by e-mail which nullifies distance and time. E-mail can open interesting possibilities for innovation across a group, by allowing people to work together over long distances and not engage in fatiguing travel. It can enhance the frequency and ease of communication both within and between firms and therefore help to strengthen relationships.

REFERENCES

1 Lester, R.K. (1998) *The Productive Edge: How U.S. Industries are Pointing the Way to a New Era of Economic Growth*. New York: W.W. Norton, p. 207.

2 Blinder, A.S. (ed.) (1990) *Paying for Productivity: A Look at the Evidence*. Washington, DC: The Brookings Institution.

3 Kohn, A. (1993) 'Why Incentive Plans Cannot Work'. *Harvard Business Review* 11: Issue 5, September–October.

Introduction:
The Value of Trust

THE NEW ECONOMY AND CIVIL SOCIETY

Corporate success has never been more dependent on the contribution of first-rate people. The new economy, typified by global competition and e-business in all its forms, has changed the rules of the game, and the speed at which the game is played. If stock market values are to be maintained, then every instrument available to managers must be brought to bear on creating an atmosphere in which innovation and excellent service prevail. The intangible assets of the firm, including people's willingness to give more of themselves, are now more significant to competition. Mining the passion and the intrinsic value of what people have to offer becomes a new asset in competition. The energy, knowledge and creativity of people as a form of capital have never had higher value. Now, more than ever before, trust is a vital asset for gaining competitive advantage. It can release the energy to succeed.

'You can blather on endlessly about teamwork and trust, but if your people don't see what's in it for them, don't expect them to listen,' wrote a contributor to *Fortune*. They had run a story in 1989 called 'The Trust Gap', but by 1996 found that the gap had widened in the intervening seven years, despite the flattening of many hierarchies in corporate America. 'To reach out across the trust canyon to find and instill shared values, you have to understand how value systems work . . . people don't buy corporate values, they roll their own.'[1]

Trust enlarges the scope for action on any playing field. It can enhance the capacity of a new leader. The trusted leader has a great asset in relying on relationships and support which can be renewed with little effort. A leader without trust may seem self-serving and manipulative. Trust can create a significant and positive atmosphere in negotiation where trust, no matter how grudging at the outset, can develop by meeting and talking over and over again. Trust can ensure positive working relationships encouraging people to commit themselves whole-heartedly at work and 'go that extra mile'. Once released, the energy which is created can be converted into value. Trust has been a vital ingredient to successful mergers and strategic alliances, as low trust has marked out many failures in mergers and alliances in the 1990s. Trust has always been the foundation of successful client relationships. Now it has been recognized that trust will be a key differentiator, determining the success or failure of web-based marketing. Security break-downs, non-fulfilment of orders and misuse of customer information in well-publicized instances have seriously damaged confidence. 'Trust will soon become the currency of the Internet,' wrote several researchers recently.[2]

If the modern corporation is one of the great achievements of the twentieth century, the biggest challenge ahead is how to engage people at work. Recruitment and retention of key people is at a premium, and companies are competing with each other over share option schemes and bonus packages. But in the United States 25 million people have already opted out of the corporate economy to operate as free agents in the network economy. Keeping people is at a premium.[3] High-profile employers such as investment banks and consulting firms were recently losing out to small entrepreneurial e-business start-ups. The competition for people through reward alone can be costly, as bonus and share option payments escalate. The next generation of key people in business may be looking for something in addition to pay, when the competition for talent through reward runs its course. Beyond the high water mark of reward stimulated by marketplace competition, there will still be the need to motivate people and build commitment.

The rush to give highly valued people a stake in the profitability of the firm has created a new form of competition. But if firms are competing only on the price of people, all profit sharing does is to add loyalty (however temporary) to the transaction costs of employment. Share options and profit sharing are key extrinsic rewards. Less obvious but no less important are the intrinsic factors of how each firm considers autonomy and ownership of a job and its contribution towards employability in the marketplace. Each of these can lead to a commitment and passion which is based on trust.

Models of change, tools and techniques developed throughout the 1990s have been successfully implemented by only a small number of highly successful organizations. Called 'the living company' or 'built to last',[4] these show excellent return on shareholder value as well as taking people issues seriously. The 'lap of honour' belonged to companies such as Hewlett-Packard, Motorola and Levi Strauss. But even these have had difficulties of late: HP has restructured; Motorola has lost considerable shareholder value and Levi Strauss closed several US factories in 1997, making 6400 people redundant. Who will take their place in the years to come as excellent working relationships become more and more significant?

The management of change and restructuring of businesses with re-engineering or downsizing were done rapidly and largely unsuccessfully in the 1990s. There remains great untapped potential in most enterprises today. Industry leaders such as Jack Welch of GE and Percy Barnevik, formerly of ABB, have often said that they could not make a significant impact if their people were giving only a fraction of what they had to offer.[5] There is a lesson here for all business leaders.

Restructuring and re-engineering were the norm in the 1990s. Looking back on this decade of effort, the financial and non-financial evidence does not seem to have justified the cost. There is no evidence that the wave of corporate restructuring and downsizing made any significant overall contribution to productivity either in the United States or in Britain. Re-engineering and restructuring based on downsizing added little to productivity, which remained dogged by underperformance.[6] Campaigns such as Total Quality Management and re-engineering seemed to have forgotten about 'the people'. Productivity is still a major issue. Strategies for operational effectiveness – such as process improvement, re-engineering or TQM – also had little effect on productivity. Now we are still trying to build it.

Some firms created independent profit centres, and fragmented organizations into a series of semi-independent businesses or divisions responsible for their own P&L. Rather than attack productivity, these profit centres brought high transaction costs within the firm, with duplication which added to the waste of corporate resources. Hewlett-Packard had become a benchmark of excellent human resource practices based on the 'HP Way'. The culture was created in the early days when – together with Apple computers – they became one of the first generation of Silicon Valley enterprises. But in 1999 when Carli Fiorini took over as chief executive, she restructured the firm to cut the cost of duplication found in the separate profit centres to try to return to better collaboration across product lines.

No single pattern of employment relations will dominate in the years to come. Each enterprise has a choice of how to develop a policy for the retention of its people. These policies are naturally linked to the firm's strategic resources and its deployment of other key assets like technology or capital. All share option schemes are replicable. People may choose to leave for incremental benefit.

In the United States and Britain, some have taken the 'high ground' and advocated that public policy should help shape the outcome of relations at work. They argue for the spread of high trust, high commitment and the high-performance workplace. The Third Way, an old term relaunched by the policy publicist, Will Hutton in 1997, is an attempt to reintroduce mutuality in civil society.[7] The debate about the Third Way is intended to overcome the (perceived) decline of sociability. The decline of social capital and voluntarism was obvious during the Thatcher–Reagan years of the 1980s, and a return to building civil society became a major preoccupation. Mutuality has become a buzzword which reflects collective self-organization, a sense of membership, reciprocity and rights.[8] In practice, it is the way in which community can assist in the improvement of education, health and social welfare, based on trying to engage the private sector in shared schemes.

Government and enterprise are currently grappling with the implications of the new economy which redefines competitive advantage. The debates and discussions on the new economy come after an unfinished debate on civil society. In the last decade of the twentieth century several scholars were preoccupied with the decline of trust and its implications for civil society. The pioneering historical work by Robert Putnam had us worried because of the decline of social activity, typified by bowling clubs in the United States, while conservative theorists like Francis Fukuyama warned us that the Chinese would never succeed because they never had bowling clubs in the first place.[9] Putnam argues that Americans have seen the collapse of honesty and trust in which citizens benefit from shared networks and reliance on one another. It is in crisis because of the 'go-it-alone society'. 'Even Adam Smith argued that the market depended on sympathy. Erode that sympathy and you risk destroying the basis of trust on which the dealings of the market ultimately depend.'[10] Research in the United States claims to have found a relationship between high trust societies and high-performing societies. The work concludes that when societies act as mere distributive mechanisms between narrow interest groups, a decline in civic-mindedness can reduce material well-being, and that this decline may detract from innovation which is a vital component of competitive advantage.[11]

UNDERSTANDING TRUST

The trust we are willing to entertain is formed initially in the family environment based on the experiences of youth. It may be reflected, fostered or discouraged in the institutions in which we participate later in life — be they civic, social, occupational or professional. We begin to develop a clear assessment of those whom we trust, and whom we do not trust. We know that we are still judging people each day to assess our measure of potential trust.

The lack of trust in oneself is a kind of fear that one does not have the ability or capacity to face anything which is unexpected, not planned, controlled or predictable. Healthy self-respect and self trust allows a person to become a prime mover, responsible for determining his or her own fate. Creativity and innovation depend on self trust or the ability to tolerate ambiguity.[12] Successful leaders must have a great deal of self trust to deal with the uncertainties of the current business environment.

Myths about the creative process in business are that the breakthroughs depend on solitary flamboyant individuals and that creativity cannot be managed. By contrast, creativity can be developed incrementally (redesigned equipment, derivative or follow-on products) by a team, if it has the right composition. Central to creativity are passion, pride, commitment and ownership – all factors which can be generated by trust. There are many ways to encourage trust from the outset which include removing the barriers to creativity, managing diversity and giving the creative team sufficient time. There is a strong relationship between motivation and creativity.[13]

An important ingredient of creativity is openness. Great breakthroughs occur when one crosses the boundaries from one's own preoccupations to what others are focusing on. Cross-pollination is an important stimulus of creativity. Well-set boundaries define extensive possibilities. Trust makes a significant contribution to the release of creativity and innovation in an organization.[14] Jan Carlson transformed SAS (Scandinavian Air Services) from a technology-dominated bureaucracy to a customer-obsessed company run by empowered front-line personnel. Building trust was an essential part of this exercise.

Some companies are able to stimulate creativity and initiative among employees more effectively than others, pushing decision making down into the organization is only a part of what is needed. 3M and Hewlett-Packard have outstanding reputations for fostering innovative activity by encouraging employees to take 10% of their time on their own projects. This was the origin of the ubiquitous 'Post-it Note' from 3M, now a multi-million-dollar product. Once ideas for new products and services reach the approval of a special board, they are given funds for further development The chief executive of 3M, Livio DeSimone, said of his firm recently:

> Senior management's primary role is to create an internal environment in which people understand and value our way of operating . . . Our job is one of creation and destruction – supporting individual initiative

while breaking down bureaucracy and cynicism. ... It all depends on developing a personal trust relationship between those at the top and those at the lower levels. ... Supporting entrepreneurial activity depends heavily on management's ability to trust people. Some of our lab people don't see managers for six months at a time. ... A couple of years ago we redirected ourselves to hiring people who intuitively understand the discipline of the marketplace.[15]

The director of IBM Research developed guidelines for his people which included underdefining jobs, not overmapping the journey and pairing visionaries with implementers.[16] All these factors would help to develop individual self trust and trust across boundaries in an organization. They are based on trying to promote intrinsic motivation or self-driven and sustaining commitment. Intrinsic motivation goes hand in hand with high levels of satisfaction – self-actualization, in particular.

In the business world, mergers and acquisitions are no less popular, even though so many of them have failed and those which have succeeded had little impact on shareholder value. In early 2000, Germany's two largest banks – Deutche and Dresdener – had a go at trying to become a mega-corporation. The eleventh-hour break-up (not the first by any means) illustrated a failure to come to an agreement on the future of investment banking in each of the organizations. Instead of creating a mega-European bank, capable of competing with American ascendancy in investment banking globally (nine out of ten top players), the negotiations ended in bitterness and acrimony. The break-up of the BT/MCI merger a few years earlier was a failure to understand that two radically different corporate cultures cannot be joined in the same blockbuster institution without carefully testing the water and building trust little by little. BT and MCI failed miserably in their effort to build compatibility of outlook or mutual trust.

Strategic alliances, on the other hand, yield significantly higher than average returns. The traps to avoid in developing a successful alliance include failing to select the right partner or agree on goals or objectives. Without a sufficient understanding of each others' goals and expectations any partnership can easily be diverted.[17] Alliance networks can serve as conduits for sharing privileged information. Credibility and honesty in this process needs to be based on trust. As the level of mutual understanding and trust increases and the strategic partners become more comfortable with the uncertainties of the alliance, commitment builds value.[18]

Building trust in negotiations gives us a hothouse of evidence on the complexity of this issue. Since negotiators customarily feel that their counterparts are acting in a self-interested way, each party tends to be sceptical. A well-managed negotiation process can, however, be a way of building trust rather than awarding the least cost or 'winner take all' approach. Compromise itself can begin to develop trust. The most successful negotiators rely on their influencing skills to understand the other side. This form of empathy can be a powerful tool, whether used explicitly, if the situation is right, or used to develop an even more powerful and informed position for one's own side.

The firm is a social community specializing in speed and efficiency in the creation and transfer of knowledge. 'The amount that people care, trust and engage themselves at work has not only a direct effect on the bottom line, but the most direct effect of any factor on a company's lifespan.'[19] Social capital has become a popular term to identify the value of relationships in a firm, on a par with human or financial capital. Social capital can help create trust because it increases the efficiency of action, diminishes opportunism and reduces the need for costly monitoring. It can become a critical performance factor, as it focuses on the value a manager or employee adds through his or her network of contacts with other people. This view of the firm contrasts sharply with the traditional view of economists who define actions in a firm on the basis of transaction cost alone, assuming that opportunism is the norm.

A firm's capacity to invest and manage its activities in many different countries can promote innovation in different locations through its own internal network more effectively than in the marketplace. The successful multinational corporation for some is a differentiated network rather than a hub-and-spoke model. The need for worldwide learning to create adopt and diffuse new innovations depends on the richness of networks within the firm based on social capital.[20]

In the aftermath of downsizing and restructuring in the 1990s a new social contract was proposed to replace job security in some firms. Based on employability, it assumes that people will be part of a development programme including training and skills which will equip them better for the job market. The new social contract applied to professional and higher technical grades hardly touches the ordinary skilled or non-skilled worker. Since employee protection has deteriorated, fairness becomes a new asset based on a portfolio of incentives. But this form of employability is still only limited in its application.

Trust is a resource on a par with other forms of capital. Trust replaces loyalty as a primary bond. The traditional loyalty of the past often stands in the way of building competitive strength[21] because it is much less agile and resilient in the competitive climate of business today. This book looks at more than just the simple award of trust, by considering the situational basis of trust, or situations which may be characterized by trust or low trust. It asks the reader to consider the value of collaboration and cooperation as assets themselves.

Corporate boards have recently begun to recognize the significance of trust – sometimes adding it to values and mission statements of the organization. But before trust becomes another managerial cliché without any real understanding, let us look try to see how it might become a working concept, an asset in the modern organization. Trust has appeared as a corporate value in annual reports as diverse as those from the Lippo Bank of Indonesia, Electrolux of Sweden and Sun Microsystems of California. Clearly we are dealing with an idea which has strong global resonance – perhaps universality – in the world of work.

Despite considerable public debate on the decline of trust and civic-mindedness and their potential for increasing the cost of business and service delivery, there is hardly a consensus on the meaning of trust or an understanding of the consequences of low trust. General diagnosis about trust and low trust is plentiful, but clear explanatory work on how trust can be developed, its value to an organization, and the cost of low trust remains at best elusive. Many of the existing models are inadequate, as they are lab-derived and unrelated to real situations.

People are talking about trust in public life and business. It has become a buzzword and seems destined to remain so. Sceptics have sharpened their wits wondering if politicians and managers only use trust as a public relations formula to cover the more intractable problems of governance – particularly those with a clear and formidable challenge like healthcare and pay and conditions. Some people will never cede the position of unmitigated self-interest as a guiding concept, content to measure relationships for their transactional content alone. This was the basis of years of adversarial strife in industrial relations in Europe and North America as well as ever-growing disillusion with the political process.

CHAPTER SUMMARY

This book will first demonstrate the centrality of trust to competitive advantage by revealing its power for creating value and energy. It will indicate how distrust or low trust can destroy these vital qualities. Responding to managers who have often told me how they have experienced the destructive power of low trust, the second aim is a practical one. This book will help people understand how to take action to overcome low trust, how to begin to build trust and sustain it over time. *Trust* aims to rescue the term from its vague position of approval without reflection.

The book will attempt to make trust a practical and workable objective for managers, by clarifying basic concepts and giving key indicators for action. Making trust a practical term begins with a consideration of the conditions under which people are likely to award trust, or the environment which may become a trusting one. Trust appears to be complex and elusive. Most of the academic research remains beyond the reach of people who recognize the severe decline of trust at work and would like to try to grapple with its consequences immediately. They seem to be able to see and feel low trust. They have begun to consider its cost. They are less certain how to tackle its consequences.

The book will argue that trust has value and can make an important contribution to competitive performance. It is not a case for harmonious work relations or 'being nice to workers'. Trust can become an important calculable asset. The book discusses the conditions under which people are willing to trust each other in novel circumstances, and why and on what basis people in a firm might be willing to do so.

Research was completed at a time when the contraction of the workforce shattered the traditional social contract of employment security. The drive for process and performance improvement did not generate much trust since they ignored the people factor. Perhaps the most dramatic repudiation of the traditional contract between employee and employer was in the IBM experience – shedding 200 000 people over eight years. Many firms have experienced less dramatic shrinkage, but often with no less dramatic consequences for trust. In most of the organizations, the old social contract and the old approach to employment were not altered to help people understand the changes or cope with the consequences. People in the organization who were threatened rarely had an alternative model or even a campaign on which to build a new outlook.

For many organizations 'downsizing' was a matter of cutting cost out of product or service delivery. It seems to have had very little impact on productivity. It created a powerful drag on employee morale. How much expenditure removed was later sacrificed to the cost of lower motivation, shirking, time wasting, poor performance is difficult to assess. Research has demonstrated that 'employees who survived downsizing trust management less and are therefore less likely to cooperate with them in the future'. The impact of diminished trust is an important consideration.[22] Some firms used the opportunity to reduce numbers at the same time as building a new approach to strategy and employment. This at least helped people to understand their position.

This book is in three parts. Part I (Chapters 1–4) states the argument in general terms. Part II (Chapters 5–10) groups case studies of firms which were developing performance improvement and presents the empirical research on which the general argument is based. Part III includes a chapter on collaborative capital in the realm of investment banks and concludes with Chapter 12 on the trusted leader with a consideration of the strategic asset of trust.

Stating the centrepiece argument of the book, *Chapter 1* defines trust and identifies its dynamic quality. It outlines the cost of low trust and summarizes research on the development and maintenance of trust. It relates trust to traditional people issues and the need for trust in the quest for competitive advantage.

Chapter 2 looks at trust as an equity and considers why it is more versatile than loyalty in the current competitive climate. It looks at how trust can be built in an organization. Information is crucial to building trust, and trust gains value through management consistency. Two types of information are significant for building trust: disclosure information and process or micro information. Trust is difficult to measure since it cannot easily be unravelled from a complex set of social relationships in a firm. The chapter considers different forms of collaboration, including cooperation, participation and involvement and two types of trust: mutual and discretionary. It traces how mutual trust develops in three stages and identifies the building blocks of trust. The factors which are critical to the development of trust are communication, openness, fairness, recognition, care and concern. Finally the chapter considers the relationship between trust and reputation.

Chapter 3 considers why employee participation may not be enough to build the type of commitment essential to performance improvement. It demonstrates how openness, fairness and recognition are all factors which affirm trust and make it more secure. This chapter summarizes the results of the questionnaire survey of more than 1000 employees – finding much attention devoted to understanding performance improvement. Little enough attention is given to improving the work context, the environment in which employees may be willing to give more of themselves to the work process (or not).

Chapter 4 looks at learning and alignment. People simply need to know where they fit into the organization and what is the specific contribution they make to the goals of the enterprise. The consistency and credibility of management were found to be of critical significance to building trust and fostering alignment, as well as constant communication on a regular basis. Tacit knowledge or the 'how' things are done, the 'learning by doing' component of knowledge, is crucial to performance improvement. People were willing to provide their tacit knowledge to improved performance and process innovation – often a critical contribution, if they understood their contribution and felt recognized for it. Tacit knowledge (often used in the context of innovation and the development of technology) is a concept of very recent application to the embedded knowledge of the front-line employee.

Chapters 5–10 are case studies of how trust develops or fails to develop, and the impact it has on performance improvement. *Chapter 5* is based on a high trust firm – ICL Manufacturing, which became the independent company Design to Distribution in 1994 – a remarkable turnaround and high achievement in an exceedingly competitive industry, where margins were continuously reduced, lead-times shortened and where market imperatives often left jobs insecure.

Chapter 6 considers a company which experimented with many changes in strategy, structure and process, leaving its employees with little consistent direction and a serious lack of alignment. Although there was great promise and anticipation of getting long-standing employees involved in performance improvement, they were concerned that 'it would go the way of all the previous efforts'. The chapter will consider the potential loss of trust in senior management in particular, through frequent cycles of restructuring, downsizing and policy changes, and map the potential effects this loss had on the organization.

Chapter 7 is based on a low trust firm which (although trying new forms of organizational change) was beset by very poor communication and low employee confidence in management. The firm tried to introduce employee involvement through a training programme, but failed because the traditional adversarial relationship between management and employees remained strong. Each attempt to try to develop a new approach and improve the culture was dogged by uncertain steps and contradictory efforts. This chapter will trace the initial efforts to try to change the organization and outline systematically what went wrong.

Chapter 8 gives an example of another chronically low trust firm, which introduced a quality programme based on employee involvement that foundered in the traditional atmosphere of the firm. Major problems could be attributed to the lack of a time frame or impetus for change. The new structures failed to be embedded in the unchanged hierarchy. The inadequacy of communication was one of the major issues, combined with a lack of encouragement and inadequate team briefs. The quality training programme was not properly introduced, leading to an atmosphere rife with rumours. Management was seen to have a succession of enthusiasms in which they did not truly engage themselves, according to employees. Since it was in the defence industry the plant had a complex paper trail and an opaque organization. The supervisors who led the process improvement programme remained autocratic, and the unions called one-day strikes whenever new work processes were introduced.

Chapter 9 tells the story of several attempts to generate performance improvement – some successful, some less so – and the impact of trust on these. The firm made considerable strides in trying to develop changes in the organization which could begin to foster trust. There are some illustrative examples of why this had been successful, and why it had not. In this chapter we revisit the concept of alignment, trying to explain why disjointed or discontinuous efforts do not generate sustainable change.

Chapter 10 is an example of a firm which made great strides in changing the production processes but found it difficult to change its traditional culture. The general manager of this company tried to rally support with a direct appeal to the workforce. The hierarchical structure was dismantled. Introducing a new production system (based on a Japanese model) was the impetus for change. The extent of organizational transformation was impressive. People were keen to get involved with the new practices. Flexible working practices were introduced. A fundamental question, however, remained about the change in the culture. There was little successful liaison between front-line workers and technical and engineering staff. A 'them and us' culture prevailed, despite the changes.

Chapter 11 steps away from front-line involvement and looks at the opportunity to build collaborative capital and client loyalty in investment banks, arguing that this is a valuable competitive asset for the future. Capital ratings may not be the only measure of success. Following a decade of conglomeration, investment banks are now looking at ways of enhancing their internal capital. The chapter looks at the different approaches in US and European firms and identifies different types of networking to promote and support global business. It takes on the issue of operational risk and considers the prospect for creating new values among the staff. Focusing on clients rather than deals may be the impetus for change from the star system which has been dominant until now. The complex portfolios of clients call for significant new forms of teamwork and collaboration. But the most difficult step may be the one which turns the attention of senior management from short-term deal making to longer-term transformation and mutual reward.

Chapter 12 is a conclusion which looks again at the contribution of trust to competitive advantage and returns to some of the major themes of the book. It begins with a brief study of the qualities of the trusted leader, a new style of leadership needed in the current climate of business. Trust helps to foster the legitimacy of the leader. In appealing for trust, a leader demonstrates self trust and encourages the creation of an environment in which others can follow his lead. Leadership focuses on values. As the guardian of the corporate strategy, the leader is the storykeeper and storyteller. The chapter illustrates how managers might make more of the opportunity to create long-lasting trust, while considering commitment to shareholder value. Finally, it links these to the prospects for keeping the momentum going, for using trust to strengthen the pace of change.

REFERENCES

1 Stewart, T.A. (1996) 'Why Value Statements Don't Work'. *Fortune*. 10 June.
2 Urban, G., F. Sultan and W. Qualls (2000) 'Placing Trust at the Center of your Internet Strategy'. *Sloan Management Review* 42: No. 1, Fall, 48.
3 Hutton, W. and J. Knell (2000) 'Born Free'. *Financial Times* 26 July, 13.
4 de Geus, A. (1999) *The Living Company* London: Nicholas Brearley; Porras, J.I. and J.C. Collins (1995) *Built to Last: Successful Habits of Visionary Companies*. New York: Century Books.
5 Bartlet, C.A. and S. Ghoshal (1998) *The Individualised Corporation*. Boston, MA: Harvard Business School Press, 7–8.

6 Lester, R.K. (1998) *The Productive Edge: How Industries are Pointing the Way to a New Era of Economic Growth.* New York: W.W. Norton.

7 Hutton, W. (1997) *The State to Come.* London: Vintage.

8 Leadbetter, C. (1997) *Civic Spirit: The Big Idea for a New Political Era.* London: Demos.

9 Putnam, R.D. (1995) 'Bowling Alone: America's Declining Social Capital'. *Journal of Democracy* No. 6: 65–78; Fukuyama, F. (1995) *Trust: The Social Virtues and the Creation of Prosperity.* London: Hamish Hamilton.

10 Handy, C. (2001) 'Tocqueville Revisited: The Meaning of American Prosperity'. *Harvard Business Review* January: 60.

11 Knack, S. and P. Keefer (1996) 'Does Social Capital Have an Economic Payoff? A Cross-Country Investigation'. Center for Institutional Reform, University of Maryland, Working Paper 197, July.

12 Maslow, A.H. (1998) *Maslow on Management.* London and New York: John Wiley, 27, 226, 230.

13 Leonard, D. and W. Swap (1999) *When Sparks Fly: Igniting Creativity in Groups.* Boston, MA: Harvard Business School Press, 1–6, 20, 91, 176.

14 Kao, J. (1996) *Jamming: The Art and Discipline of Business Creativity.* New York: HarperBusiness, 61, 90.

15 'How Can Big Companies Keep the Entrepreneurial Spirit Alive?' (1995) *Harvard Business Review* November–December: 184.

16 Horn, P. (1997) 'A Personal View: Creativity and the Bottom Line'. *Financial Times* 17 November, 12.

17 Harbison, J.R. and P. Pekar Jr. (1998) *Cross-Border Alliances in the Age of Collaboration.* New York: Booz Allen Hamilton.

18 Doz, Y.L. and G. Hamel (1998) *Alliance Advantage: The Art of Creating Value through Partnership.* Boston, MA: Harvard Business School Press, 22, 223.

19 de Geus, A. *op. cit.*, p. 18.

20 Nohria, N. and S. Ghoshal (1997) *The Differentiated Network: Organizing Multinationals for Value Creation.* San Francisco, CA: Jossey-Bass, 4, 10.

21 Shaw, R.B. (1997) *Trust in the Balance.* San Francisco, CA: Jossey-Bass, 204, 206

22 Sull, D. and N. Nohria (1995) 'Managing Distrust: The Hidden Cost of Downsizing'. In *Downsizing: Management Demands and Ethical Dilemmas*, edited by A. Ras Joshi and G. Nelson. Boston, MA: Harvard Business School Press, 74.

Part I

The chapters in the first part of this book consider several different facets of trust. Trust is seen as a form of capital, essential to competitive advantage in the new economy and the rapidly changing business environment. This book focuses on trust in the relations between employees and management. Understanding the significance of trust in the business world would also have us look at negotiations, mergers, acquisitions and strategic alliances. In the firm, we argue that trust is important for the development of creativity and innovation and the devolution of responsibility.

This book evolved from a story about creating commitment at work to a statement about the centrality of trust. We define mutual trust as confident expectation. We consider the cost of low trust including fraud, controls, fear, uncertainty and a loss of energy, momentum and value. We note that people seem to be willing to award trust on the basis of fair treatment, respect and recognition for the contribution they make. We also note that deference to authority in an organization is often based more on trust than on competence, particularly for those who are some distance in grade from senior management. It takes time to establish trust, but once established it can be renewed with little effort.

Trust may be considered an equity which can yield a long-term return. By contrast, loyalty is not as resilient and robust as trust and it can be the enemy of change. The building blocks of trust include information and communication in a form which can be readily understood. Openness, fairness and recognition encourage the development of trust. Trust is sustained by reputation which is based on both competence and consistency of management actions and style.

Trust enhances the social capital in a firm by strengthening relationships. Our survey of over 1000 front-line employees demonstrates how the firms which participated in the research built an awareness of performance improvement based on quality while neglecting trust. While people were informed about the quality campaign and while they were willing to make a significant effort to support it, only about half felt that they had a voice in the process and a very small proportion felt that top management had a sincere interest in their welfare or could be counted on to offer a fair deal. The effects of these attitudes are traced in the in-depth case studies in Part II of the book.

Building trust is very close to learning and alignment in an organization. If employees feel that they can make a difference and are willing to contribute to performance improvement, they may offer their tacit knowledge — that which has been learned on the job. There are several case studies of successful and unsuccessful learning working around such themes as leadership, communication and management commitment. Three stages of learning from programmed intervention to embedded change are traced through specific cases.

Trust at Work and the Cost of Low Trust $\quad$ 1

ENGAGING PEOPLE

Competitive advantage in the new economy is based on three things, all of which require the highest degree of commitment of the people in the organization: the achievement of ambitious performance targets; the capacity to rearrange goals quickly and resolutely; and the ability to generate fresh ideas on a continual basis. The real challenge is to maintain high energy and flexibility by encouraging people to give their best. Those firms which can mine the passion of their people will create sustainable advantage. They are clear winners. Trust is a key component of the new economy, though it remains elusive to many firms.

Engaging people at work can have a vital impact on retention. It can release innovation and creativity. The old motivational levers no longer seem to work. Studs Terkel, a legendary Chicago radio journalist – famous as a voice of the people – recorded the thoughts of people in a factory in 1972: 'Most of us on the assembly line have jobs which are too small for our spirit.'[1] Just over two decades later, Jack Welch, who had taken General Electric through a remarkable recovery by the time of his retirement as CEO in 2001, said 'Our biggest task is to redefine our relationship to our employees – to build a place where people have the freedom to be creative, where they feel some sense of accomplishment – a place which brings out the best in everybody.'[2] In the two decades which separate those observations, the pace and intensity of competition has forced us to look for new forms of capital and a complete revaluation of all assets. Trust has enormous potential, and low trust has great cost.

Bob Ayling resigned as chief executive of British Airways to 'spend more time with his family' after fourteen-hour days at the helm of what was 'the world's favourite airline'. The tabloid press could not resist: 'First King, then Marshall, now Ayling.' In his early days, Ayling pronounced his determination to create an open communicative organization. The new design of BA headquarters, completed in 1999, was built around 'hot desking' and enhanced collaboration. The first confrontation of Ayling's tenure at BA was with the pilots. Following protracted negotiations, BA settled because of strong union pressure. The second confrontation was with the cabin crew – particularly damaging because they are the front line of service to all customers who fly BA. At that juncture, service began to slip and goodwill was lost. And then there were the celebrated tail fins and the displeasure of British business-class passengers. Ayling was right to identify that 'people were his strongest asset', a familiar boardroom cliché of the 1990s, but he was typically confrontational when it came to dealing with the staff directly. And finally the trust of his board and the City reacted as the share price dipped further and further, and cost-effective reforms became difficult to achieve.

A world away from the regime of Bob Ayling at BA is the SAS Institute, the world's largest private software company, based in the USA. It stood out of the crowd among the frenzied tech flotations and dotcom fever of 1999–2000. The chief executive of SAS, Jim Goodnight, is a strong believer in attracting and retaining staff by providing an excellent working environment, a good work/life balance and pleasant perks, rather than monetary reward. After twenty-four years in business and the pressure on staff through constant attempted poaching, the founders decided to award some of the stock to employees. SAS rates as one of *Fortune*'s top employers, described as 'the closest thing to a work-er's utopia in America'.[3]

Take another example, the much larger energy company, AES, with over 30 000 employees dispersed all over the world. Founded by Dennis Bakke and Roger Sant, AES has no personnel department, public rela-tions, legal, environmental or strategic planning departments. Its four core values of integrity, fairness, social responsibility and fun are backed up by the assumptions that AES people are creative, thinking individuals, are responsible and can be held accountable. Most financial decisions, for example, are made by project teams comprised largely of people without any formal training in finance. The corporate culture came to be called a 'honeycomb', which captures the idea of relatively small, flexible inter-related teams working on different projects and activities.[4]

WHAT IS TRUST?

Trust can be defined as *confidence in the outcome of a situation*. It is a simple but powerful assumption which sustains a relationship over time. Think for a moment about personal relationships on which you can rely and how they stand apart from others. Consider their value to you. Confident expectation is shorthand for trust but more precisely, trust is *an expectation about the positive actions of other people, without being able to influence or monitor the outcome.* It is an anticipation of positive behaviour for actions of importance. To put it another way, it is a form of confidence based on a consistency of feeling rather than a continuous assessment of evidence. The supreme value of trust becomes the willingness to commit to a relationship before knowing the outcome. In the ICL/D2D plant near Manchester, the MD knew he could count on people to work weekends and long hours at short notice. Brought into the common cause of saving the business, they were right behind the effort to bring more business to the site. In this case, honest, open and frank communication paid dividends, and the consistency of action maintained trust over time.

Trust relies on an investment in relationships which become valuable in and of themselves. It reduces the necessity for an audit after each new independent action, giving the relationship itself significance. Trust increases the scope for action by shelving conflict. Trust implies risk because it is based on confidence in a relationship, or the capacity to deliver, without having to continually monitor the outcome. It is that non-monitoring of the outcome which saves enormous amounts of time. Confident expectation is useful shorthand for trust. Confident because trust allows us to believe in the positive outcome of what people are likely to do. This is

Relying on people

Anticipating a positive outcome

Being able to count on people

In short, confident expectation

Trust does not imply control

You take the risk because you trust the relationship

Trust means that you cannot control the outcome

Figure 1.1 What is trust?

important because it is based on actions over which we have no influence. We do not know the outcome, but only anticipate it on the basis of trust. We anticipate that a trusted person will do the right thing at significant times. We count on them. It is not essential to continue to assess or evaluate what people are doing on a continual basis, if you trust them. You take it on the basis of faith in the relationship. You can create spare energy for yourself by not being so concerned (see Figure 1.1).

THE DYNAMISM OF TRUST

Trust can be a critical asset. It encourages us to take a pause for a time from fixed attention on the goals and outcomes of what we are all striving to achieve, and focuses on the process of how we get there. We have spent a decade or more looking at industrial, service and technology-based process improvement. The process we may have ignored is the opportunity to create genuinely resilient relationships – a new form of social capital based on people.

Once trust is established, one can go along, tolerating the occasional dalliance, rationalizing expectations, short of questioning trust. If something dramatic happens bringing sharply different evidence to light, trust can be destroyed, with disastrous consequences. This evidence breaks that faith. Trust is slow to build; distrust comes swiftly and dramatically, as in the case of Bob Ayling at BA. These qualities of individual trust and relationships are not new. What is new is the fact that productivity depends on their transference to groups of people, institutions and more generally to the quality of civil society. This move brings into focus the process of the development of relationships as well as their contribution to the outcome of action.

Trust has value. It can grow with use. It can expand or contract over time. It is based on risk, since it is accorded on the basis of limited information. Trust may be slow to develop and fragile. It is renewable but not infinitely robust. Trust can be destroyed in an instant by a major breach and will take a long time to restore, if ever. Major negative actions are more visible, more specifically defined, more talked about, more easily sustained. An accumulation of positive events – while they may yield a significant contribution – appear less sharp or distinct, less talked about.

Trust has much greater dynamism and potential value than loyalty. Management experts and gurus alike have been saying for a long time that employees who are committed to corporate objectives, and who 'buy into' values with their hearts as well as their heads, are more diligent, productive and innovative. All the experiments with performance improvement prove that it is quite easy to generate initial participation. Getting people involved in such activities may encourage them to give more of themselves – a contribution of specific knowledge as well as initial personal commitment. Management consistency is vital to this next step – consistency in communication and action, giving employees confidence in the scope and direction of management action.

This is what took place at Rolls-Royce, with a stunning 60% increase in output following a radical redesign of the organization from 1996 to 1999. Rolls-Royce invited the 20 000 employees to enter a company programme designed to generate debate about the future shape of the organization. A total of 5000 managers went through a leadership programme organized in collaboration with the consultancy, A.T. Kearney.

Foremen were replaced by coaches. A fitter with eighteen years' experience of Rolls-Royce said:

> The foremen used to be supervisors and dish out the jobs. Now we are doing it ourselves. As coaches, they are more like trainers. We're far more involved in the job. It gives you more interest. When it started no one wanted it. It was the thought of change more than anything else, to be honest. But it's here. It's the best thing since sliced bread. I love it.[5]

Firms which introduced empowerment and then failed to give people responsibility for their work and results created confusion. In the 1980s and 1990s, firms went through many paradigms, models and techniques, yet the undertow of poor results, or sidelining of major achievements, proved that something more was needed. There is a high proportion of untapped energy in almost every business. Those who can mine it in the future will find themselves ahead of the pack. Some are looking for the soul of the corporation, its purpose or testing the versatility of the 'glue' which holds it together, or 'the smell of the place.' What they may be missing is something more fundamental – which can be created step by step.

High-performing firms which deliver continual shareholder value, or those which have transformed themselves and created sustainability, have found that there is remarkable potential energy in working successfully together. The energy generated by trust is much more than a sum of individual contributions, offering higher value than multiples of individual contributions. Trust yields a compound return simply because it allows relationships to be renewed with little or no effort. A manager who can count on the rapid introduction of a new directive or target, or change a process to take on a new client with little extra effort, has a significant asset. He can count on his people. This resilience can enlarge the scope for doing things with little extra effort. It enlarges the playing field of action by reducing the penalty zone.

As a form of capital, trust is renewable with little effort. It encourages people to 'go that extra mile' and offer more of themselves. Trust is the base substance of creativity and innovation – the capacity to create 'a buzz', or sustain a flow. Social capital based on trust – its constancy and renewability – may be one of the most valuable assets of the new century. In most jobs, people have been waiting for a long time to prove what they can do. Trust introduces a world based less on rights and obligations, contract and pay than on a new form of partnership. There is untapped power in the capacity to work together. Trust enables people to act on their willingness to give more of themselves.

In an organization, trust reduces friction and releases potential energy. That energy once guided by the purpose of the organization – the goals which form the basis of the strategy – becomes a form of capital to an enterprise. People need to know their role in the context of these goals. If they understand them and feel recognized for their contribution, a form of intrinsic or self-motivation can be developed. People who work well together, and spar off each other with new ideas can create a form of social capital which can itself become intrinsic to the firm.

THE COST OF LOW TRUST

Low trust, distrust and fear can add significant cost to doing business. These are at the heart of individual and interdepartmental misunderstanding. Low trust often requires costly rationalization. Mistrust bears a high cost in terms of time – meetings, memoranda and justification. Managers are usually aware of the negative cost of low trust but do not know what to do about it. In some firms, senior management appear to have insulated themselves further and further from their people, despite all the positive evidence on performance and value to the contrary. The widening salary differential between boardroom and the front line, and scandals about 'fat cat' salaries and payoffs, have created cynicism. People on the front line are shrewd in their assessment of the behaviour of people in corporate headquarters – however many layers of management lie in between. They often know all about the long knives among key personalities on the executive floor.

In the 1990s affability became a new management style. The entertainment industry boomed with skiing trips, cruise parties and charitable fun runs, while back at work the atmosphere often remained poisonous.

On a Monday morning people are cut down to size – given little way out except to blow off steam at the pub or with partners and family. It seems much easier to orchestrate affability than pause to consider the contribution of emotional intelligence. Goleman's best selling books on emotional intelligence must have been read by all the wrong people – or those seeking to cope better with a tournament culture.[6] For many at the top, emotional intelligence is after all one of those soft and fuzzy non-deliverables, like trust unable to be counted.

Low trust is the enemy of social capital and lowers the energy potential in an organization. It robs an organization of motivation and ultimately saps value. Blame makes people risk averse, reluctant to give bad news. The recent growth of 'whistle blowing' is an act of last resort. Macho management (gender neutral) is a costly activity. It has driven a wedge between financial success and fulfilment at work, which high-performing companies can ill afford. It may have been essential to the transformation of the 1980s, but it had little to offer after that – and people began to look elsewhere in the job market.

Low trust organizations can have a culture of pervasive fear, and rely on blame and control to accomplish their goals. The 'old deal' at work was based on appropriating the value of people and on short-term solutions. It carried a powerful undertow and dragged on the capacity to get things done. Fear can achieve results in the short term, but it is non-renewable and has little impact on long-term results. The reign of Arnold Weinstock at the General Electric Corporation (UK) has been critically assessed, particularly for the absence of strategic thinking or trust in his approach to management. Exclusive focus on short-term results at the expense of all else left the GEC group of companies unprepared for its future when he retired, they were incapacitated in the face of new forms of competition in the 1990s following the departure of Weinstock.[7]

Low trust requires costly rationalization. It is inefficient and destructive of the opportunities to encourage people to try to give of their best. A survey of 400 banking and healthcare employees in England in 1999 found that 23% of them had no trust in their line manager, based on ability, integrity, loyalty and openness.[8] In the boardroom of the defence

> Low trust adds significantly to the cost of doing business
>
> Low trust restricts the playing field of action
>
> Low trust is based on fear and blame saps value

Figure 1.2 The cost of low trust.

company, GEC Avionics, I once asked an Air Vice Marshall (ret.) 'When was the last time you said, "A job well done?"' Communicating blame, without any recognition of people's accomplishments, creates an environment in which people chronically underperform. When I returned six months later to Edinburgh to visit the company, he stopped me in the hallway to let me know (with a wry smile) of the considerable success he had enjoyed with this new phrase in his management toolkit. It led me to wonder how many managers in other companies might have enjoyed the same conversation to excellent effect (see Figure 1.2).

The decline of trust has become costly in financial services. Business abuses in the 1980s and 1990s on Wall Street and the City of London including the crash of the empire of Robert Maxwell generated stricter legislation on fraud, pension funds and self-policing internal IT systems demanded by the US Treasury and the Bank of England. The cost of low trust became obvious and had a high price tag. Low trust increases the cost of doing business because of the need for surveillance and control mechanisms which dedicated wrongdoers will find easy to ignore, in any case. Rogue trading and a damaged reputation can inflict greater harm on a business than the most powerful earthquake or hurricane. Fraud has been calculated to cost British companies about 6% of turnover each year. It covers a range of white-collar crimes from theft to malicious damage. White-collar crime though the Internet is on the rise. A growing awareness of fraud has resulted in the forecast growth of the international security business fourfold by 2010.[9] Fraud consultants recommend that companies create a 'risk-aware' culture.

Consider the cost of continuously resorting to rules and regulations to get things done in companies which have little common understanding. Time is costly and months of memos or meetings to try to build common ground for each new business challenge becomes an expensive affair. And no matter how extensive controls may become, one only has to consider the examples of Barings Bank and Daiwa Securities to understand how easy it is for determined people to make their own rules, when back-office controls are inadequate.

Politics and personality clashes which generate low trust are also very costly. In the boardroom at least these are customarily held in check by discretion and secrecy. The problems are known to those around the board, the well-informed press, and make work for executive counsellors. Occasionally, though, the jousting becomes public, as it did in the case of Cable & Wireless a few years ago. Executive decisions nearly ground to a halt because of the acute animosity between its chairman and chief executive. Both were voted out by the board and a new team was hired.

A chief executive who generates and maintains trust in an organization can simply do more, more flexibly, more effectively and at less cost. Think of the enhancement of leadership capacity in an organization in which people understand where the leader is headed and are willing to follow him. Consider the decentralization of authority to front-line people with clear, strong, shared operating principles based on trust. Trust enables people to do more; low trust limits what they can achieve. This is a heavy cost in a highly competitive world.

> Leaders and employee owners at Republic Engineered Steels in Ohio recognized that the hourly and salaried employees had been operating for years under this kind of 'institutionalized' distrust. As a steel manufacturer, Republic was starting with a traditional industrial environment that was built on mistrust. 'Don't trust those guys; they always watch out for their own interests' is what you learned when entering the ranks of one of these groups. Each time that some-one did something that appeared to be 'in their interest' the wall of distrust was built a little higher. To be successful, this company had to bring down the walls of mistrust. Theoretically, employee ownership creates a situation where operating 'in your own interest' is in everyone's common

interest. But reality shows us that people must first learn how to trust each other before they can effectively work towards common goals.[10]

In an atmosphere of low trust, risk avoidance and aversion to new ideas – both based on the fear of making a mistake – are a considerable cost. Risk avoidance can lead to skilful attempts to hide data and information for fear of being blamed. Regular control regimes often promote such skill and stealth to a fine art. Risk avoidance on a large scale can create paralysis in an organization. It would appear safer to do nothing rather than try out new ideas. Thinking 'out of the box' is completely ruled out. A testing question is whether or not senior management can create an environment in which it is possible to convey bad news.

> As they were driving to work on March 7, Ciba Geigy employees heard on their car radios about an impending merger between their company and Sandoz Ltd, another Swiss pharmaceutical giant. No information was provided on how the merger would affect employees – only that workforce reductions of at least 10% were expected. Employees arrived at work anxious and bewildered.
>
> If management couldn't trust them with such vital information, how could employees trust management to look out for their interests once the merger occurred? The fact that high-level mergers are rarely announced to employees ahead of time was hardly reassuring. Good news or bad, employees should be able to trust management to give it to them straight, to mean what is said and to always follow through on promises.[11]

When senior management do not convey bad news openly and honestly (and it is not provided in a radio broadcast) the quality of information which filters down from the top is always suspect. Risk avoidance can be linked to complacency – the 'fat and lazy' syndrome – found in some of the world's dominant companies at one time or another. Companies such as IBM, General Motors and Kodak have all had to come to terms with damaging complacency. Inward focus is typical of such organizations, making them unresponsive to new trends and innovations, which ultimately overtake them in the marketplace. Remaining strategically alert and organizationally flexible in the face of attack from the outside requires trust (see Figure 1.3).

Fraud

Controls

Uncertainty

Fear

Defensive behaviour

Blame culture

Excessive politics

Competition rather than collaboration

Tournament culture

Retention problems

Loss of energy and momentum

Loss of value

Figure 1.3 Low trust in the corporation.

If people are offering only 30% or even 60% of their potential, value has been lost. Or they give their all while the boss is hovering – but perhaps never travel that 'extra mile' which they know may really make a difference. And at the earliest possible opportunity, they exit for new opportunities, while the cost of recruitment and replacement adds up. In the current climate of competition we need more than that. Studs Terkel's assembly-line worker of the 1970s gives us an idea of how much more people are willing to give ('to recover their spirit'). While technology, delivery systems, return on capital are key assets which are easier to fit, measure and fix, the underperformance of people in an organization can have the most devastating consequences. That it is difficult to measure makes it no less important.

What is more easily measurable is the cost of low trust – expenditure on increasingly elaborate control systems, the annual national bill for fraud, jobs which invite risk aversion and encourage people to keep their heads down, and the reluctance to give bad news. Trust thrives on clear boundaries and responsibilities without external controls. Uncertainty and fuzziness are its enemies. It may seem obvious to introduce a control system, rather than clear up the chaos and uncertainty in which people work. Clearing up is a longer-term investment in a process which is bound to pay long-term dividends.

THE DURABILITY OF TRUST: SOME FINDINGS

Recent American research on trust has begun to clarify several important issues about trust. Some of the basic propositions are summarized here in order to bring them to the attention of managers grappling with the consequences of low trust.

- **People seem willing to award trust on the basis of fair treatment, respect and recognition for the contribution they make.** People seem to care about fair treatment because they derive a sense of identity from it – most particularly perhaps those people at the bottom of the organization who have low status and little power. Managers will be granted trust if they assist individuals in maintaining a positive self-identity or provide an environment in which this can happen. Feelings of trustworthiness are strongly linked to treatment with dignity and respect.[12]
- **People at the bottom of an organization are found to be continuous and careful 'intuitive auditors' in a process of assessment of those in authority,** even on the basis of very limited information and in conditions of uncertainty. Conditions of ignorance and vulnerability go together with low trust People in low-status positions tend to be hypervigilant and ruminative processors of information. They can recall easily more trust-related incidents than people in other parts of the organization. Violations of trust have much great significance for them.[13]

- **Deference to authority has been found to be based more on trust than on competence,**[14] especially among people with little power and low status, since they would have little accurate information on how to assess competence, or award the trust customarily reserved for professional or peer relationships. Trust can be reinforced by fairness and recognition. People respond quite remarkably even to simple acts of recognition like 'a job well done'.

- **The durability of trust is based on integrity and consistency, which over time build on the basis of reputation.** Once a reputation is established, the award of trust may be easily perpetuated with a low maintenance cost. People at the bottom of the organization may be able to judge the top people shrewdly, despite their distance in organizational terms.

- **While the development of trust builds incrementally, distrust is much more catastrophic.**[15] One can often identify with certainty the event, behaviour or incident which caused the destruction of trust. It remains a bold marker following which relationships on the basis of former assumptions begin to unravel. Once trust is compromised, the effort to rebuild it is considerable. It takes more time and effort to rebuild than to build in the first place.

Most people do not work exclusively for earnings and bonuses, or more abstractly for the creation of shareholder value. Little enough of the extra value required for outstanding corporate performance is contained in the transactional or contractual aspects of work. Even the highest-earning City analyst or chief executive is probably not just an earning machine on the job. Although I hardly subscribe to the notion that work is the 'new church', it is obvious that people spend a large part of their lives at work because of expectation and commitment, sociability, achievement or genuine interest in what they are doing. It may be the current effort at transformation, customer satisfaction, achieving a new production target. Have we begun to recognize the key invisible asset of non-instrumentality or simply the generosity of the human spirit? The real achievement is in the creation of an environment which can foster it and help it flourish.

Trust is a versatile new form of capital. It pays dividends and raises the possibility of revaluing the dignity of work.

COMPETITION DEMANDS IT

New energy is essential to businesses, which needs to move swiftly with changes in the market. It can be created by engaging people throughout an enterprise – a challenge to elicit, recognize and reward ideas and solutions. The energy to win can no longer be confined to the boardroom or a few talented boffins in research and development. The people on the front line of all businesses have a host of ideas about product and process, service and customer. Airlines, computer services and e-business may have been the first to recognize this. It is gradually being acknowledged in other sectors. The competitive challenge is considerable and it requires the realization of all assets. Trust stands alongside technology, knowledge and reserves of capital as a uniquely important asset. It is the one awaiting realization.

Improving shareholder value even in the conventional sense means looking beyond the factors which appear to be in the obvious direct short-term interests of the firm – cut the workforce, squeeze suppliers and raise prices. The impact of low morale and dissatisfaction can encourage people to leave. The cost of low trust can be devastating, with the energy of the business sapped of its potential value all day every day. Companies such as HP, Procter & Gamble and Merck stressed such factors as continuity of values, investment in people and having objectives other than profit. For decades, their share outperformed the US market.

Paradoxically we have come to acknowledge that the most profitable long-established companies are not necessarily those which are primarily profit focused (HP, Lloyds TSB, Du Pont, Mitsui Siemens are examples). Their achievements are based not only on the distinction between short- and long-term value creation but also on how assets are deployed over time. All place key emphasis on the contribution of people to this effort. Established companies have demonstrated how important individual motivation and collaborative energy can be to transformation, and how great an employer reputation can be built with people who have been waiting for an opportunity to demonstrate what they can contribute. Each year in the USA, the web site, 'The 100 Best Companies to Work for in America', is visited by millions of people. Historically many companies have made spectacular showings and then collapsed. Those companies which have stayed the course operate in an environment where survival is determined by the vitality of its key relationships – with employee, partners, customers, shareholders and the public. Reputation is earned as a confirmation of trust over time. It is an asset of recurrent value.

Try the opposite. If we treat employees, customers and others in a calculating instrumental fashion, we will get the same in return. Relationships will be valued only for immediate delivery rather than longer-term gestation. It does not enable an organization to mine the potential value which can be built into the relationship – which itself becomes a source of capital.

Clients and customers can offer valued information which serves to confirm and solidify a relationship or create insight into similar clients. However sophisticated market research data mining can become, it is often the shared insight which can leverage potential value. It is reactive and can easily become commoditized as everyone has access to the same data. A relationship built on trust can ensure the continued flow of such high-value information. Employees react to new demands with high motivation. And shareholders are loyal.

- The new executive in the UK power company, National Power, realized that his team would not deliver on stretch targets if they remained in their old mode of doing what they were told. He knew that the rapid transformation of the industry required the ideas of all – and most especially the capacity for engineers, traders, accountants and planners to collaborate more effectively. He prompted them to make 'off the wall' suggestions (by saying some wild things himself – which made them uneasy). Slowly, he encouraged self trust through recognition in each of them, and they began to take risks. New ideas began to flow.

- Goldman Sachs has always known the high value of trust in long-term client relationships, many of which were built by helping to save businesses threatened by hostile takeover bids in the 1970s and 1980s. These proved to be relationships built to last. Their culture also encouraged their people to develop new forms of collaboration by developing innovative integrated products for clients ahead of the competition. In 2000, they still consider management development to be their key issue.
- On the front line of call centres, new forms of discretionary trust and responsibility help solve customer problems. In the best of companies, customers are meant to feel that they are really being cared for. NatWest Mortgage Services consistently outperforms its peers and the rest of the Group in customer service. Their telephone clerk becomes your confidante in what can be a testing process.

Trust begins with self trust. People begin to believe in themselves if they are recognized for their efforts. They can be the most high-valued front-line employee dealing with customer problems, demonstrating a caring approach and putting extra effort into solving them. People can expand their capacity and performance ability by being trusted to take decisions, not just receive orders. And their personal pride and sense of achievement can become wrapped up in these significant front-line activities, which are the most prominent face of a company. Whether people work directly with customers or are embedded deep in the process of work, the discovery of how to capture and mine the spirit of individual motivation and performance is critical to an age of highly competitive customer service.

It was a cold Saturday morning in December. Sally was on the helpline of a US health insurance company. The first call was a worried young couple in Utah. A parent had been taken gravely ill, and was in hospital. They were not certain they could find the policy documents, and were desperately concerned about the cost of intensive care and specialist medical fees. In the course of the conversation, Sally allowed herself the indulgence of comforting them in more fulsome terms than she customarily did. It was early and there were no calls waiting. The couple thanked her and said that they never realized that the company would be so caring. In their experience it was more businesslike, even impersonal.

Sally reflected swiftly on that call before the day got further underway and the lines were busy. Healthcare, Inc. had just made twenty people in her department redundant because the bulk of the call centre activities were being centralized to another city. Times were difficult, and one of the people made redundant had been an old friend. The package was not bad and several of them had found jobs in other parts of the company. Her friend had decided to start a business of her own.

The situation had been explained clearly from the beginning and the section head kept them completely informed. The general manager had come to speak to them several times to answer questions, and often joined them for lunch or coffee at which times he made things even clearer.

Sally knew about other firms where turmoil and bitterness had prevailed. Many firms in the area had been downsizing. But at Healthcare, Inc. things had been different. Her response to the troubled young couple that morning had come as second nature. She felt that the company did care about the way they made decisions and supported her. She therefore could care.

BRINGING TRUST IN FROM THE COLD

Writing about people issues has never been in short supply during the last half of the twentieth century, initially to counter the effects of Taylorism or the scientific approach to management which preceded the Second World War. For many years thereafter, organizations grappled with issues of motivation and productivity, often shifting from one 'human resource fix' to another. In the 1980s the issues were refined to take into account new demands of competition and performance improvement based on performance-related pay, employee involvement and empowerment. The literature on leadership developed as a companion library of ideas on how to get the best out of people. Both Rosabeth Moss Kanter at Harvard and Jeffrey Pfeffer at Stanford told us that there was little new to add a decade later except that wise people policies had still to be implemented. Looking around for an explanation led them to identify a key problem which was that (ignoring the pile of books on successful leadership) most managers were still reluctant to cede control sufficiently to give people the scope to allow their spirits to grow into their jobs.

We now know that performance productivity is not affected by a single progressive human resource policy, but can be shifted by a cluster of these, including such things as training and development, incentive compensation, participation and collaborative job design.[16] There is a greater effort to link human resource policies to strategy – or one might add, considered a dynamic rather than passive strategic issue.[17] Will these encourage a new approach to the world of work?

Trust releases energy as a lubricant of social relations – a way to oil the mechanism to reduce friction and thereby be less energy consuming – a basic analogy customarily favoured by economists. Once oiled, trust can generate further energy by releasing goodwill and motivation, which themselves can quicken the pace. When people are controlled or blamed repeatedly, they hold onto their potential capacity. When they are encouraged and recognized for their achievements, they tend to stretch their potential. In ICL manufacturing, an assembly-line worker recounted how she was willing to accept more responsibility (and even take home with her new worries about performance and delivery) because she felt more involved and stretched by the tasks she was undertaking. She was given discretionary trust to do a wider range of activities and make decisions about them. This chain linking trust to motivation and responsibility is a transformation from the adversity of traditional labour relations. But most significantly, it raises the level of jobs 'too small for our spirit'.

People have not only been waiting for a generation or two to demonstrate what they can deliver and how much more they are willing to contribute. To encourage and harness this potential, some firms have become much better at communicating direction and a sense of purpose than they had customarily been. Trust begins to build on a bedrock of communication and grows stronger when messages are understandable and consistent. It is solidified through the observed consistency of behaviour. Consistency can build reputation – a precious asset of very high value, not easily replicated. Having a clear sense of direction, and a consistent story communicated widely, creates the scope for action. Living and walking the talk are essential leadership qualities for maintaining trust once earned.

There has rarely been a time when the way ahead for many organizations was so potentially risky and undefined. Bill Gates has often been quoted as saying that Microsoft had only a two-year lead over its competitors – certainly even less now. At least one of Microsoft's assets to continue to reinvent the company lies with its people.

> The culture at Microsoft is still not too far away from the loosely organized world of hacker programmers. People abhor political turf battles and bureaucratic rules and procedures, unnecessary documents, or overly formalized modes of communication, such as through a management hierarchy, written memos or publicly held meetings. As a result, individuals and teams act quickly on issues they feel are important, which is essential to solve problems and make effective adjustments quickly.[18]

Xerox went through some turbulent times redefining itself as The Document Company when its market space seemed to be so unclear nearly a decade ago, having lost so much of its copier market to Canon. It kept its people on board, however, by keeping them informed continually, however uncertain, was the strategic message. Motivation remained high.

There is power, resilience and simplicity in trust. It is a renewable asset. Trust may be of greatest value in turbulent and troubling times, but its sustainability even 'in peacetime' may be a key to maintaining the momentum of performance. As a new source of capital, trust is an intangible asset – along with knowledge, ideas, skills and organizational capabilities. Trust is as elusive, subjective and perceptual as these other highly valued invisibles. They can be forgotten when they might be most needed – during a period of rapid change. In time, there may even be some measure to tell us how precisely these contribute to shareholder value. But for the present the value of intangible assets is obvious, however difficult it is to identify and enumerate. Trust is a dynamic concept since it can generate energy. As the basis of a new form of partnership, it is a much more resilient asset than loyalty.

Creating value can be achieved on the basis of a dual-track approach, beginning with 'getting people on board', based on the strategy and purpose of the organization. Their willingness to 'go that extra mile', perhaps on the basis of progressive human resource policies, indicates that they have a significant stake in the organization.

This book evolved from a story about creating commitment at work to a statement about the centrality of trust to competitive advantage. The power of trust and its 'fit' in the time of the new economy goes together with a renewed interest in social capital in society. New management teams can be great at devaluing what has gone before – unaware of the potential for 'honouring the past'. They tend to 'slash and burn' without regard for what had gone before, perhaps still of potential value. Management fads and techniques can be most devaluing of the lifetime work of dedicated people or specialist effort. The energy created by trust develops its own value and contributes potential value to other activities, most prominently perhaps creativity, innovation and the potential for learning. It can release high-value tacit knowledge in either research or performance improvement on the shopfloor. Trust is not an end in itself. A trusting environment does not itself create value unless there are excellent ideas, strategic action and sustainability. A leader does not create trust for its own sake, but to enlarge the playing field of action.

REFERENCES

1 Terkel, S. (1977) *Working*. London: Penguin Books.
2 Ghoshal, S. and C.A. Bartlet (1998) *The Individualized Corporation*. London: Heinemann, 7–8.
3 Harvey, F. (2000) 'Of Chocolates and Profit Sharing'. *Financial Times* 26 July.
4 Pfeffer, J. (1997) 'Human Resources at AES Corporation: The Case of the Missing Department'. Graduate School of Business, Stanford University, pp. 3, 11, 15.
5 Skapinker, M. (1999) 'Rolls-Royce Flies Ahead After a Total Overhead'. *Financial Times*, 29 July, 20.

6 Goleman, D. (1996) *Emotional Intelligence*. London: Bloomsbury; Goleman, D. (1998) *Emotional Intelligence at Work*. London: Bloomsbury.

7 Brummer, A. and R. Cowe (1997) *Weinstock*. London: HarperCollins Business.

8 Clark, M. and R. Payne (1998) The Change Management Centre, Sheffield Hallam University, Sheffield, UK.

9 *Financial Times* (1998) 'Fighting Fraud'. 4 June, 12.

10 Ivancic, C. (1996) 'For Employee Owners Only'. http://www.neco.org/columns/c12.html, February.

11 Caudron, S. 'Rebuilding Employee Trust'. TIME Vista Boardroom Library, http://pathfinder.com/timesista/articles/manage/employeetrust.html

12 Tyler, T.R. and P. Dagoey (1996) 'Trust in Organizational Authorities: The Influence of Motive Attributions on Willingness to Accept Decisions'. In *Trust in Organizations*, edited by R.M. Kramer and T. Tyler, London: Sage Publications, 346.

13 Kramer, R.M. (1996) 'Divergent Realities and Convergent Disappointments in Hierarchical Relation: Trust and the Intuitive Auditor at Work'. In Kramer and Tyler, *op. cit.*, 222–227.

14 Tyler, T. and P. Degoey (1996) 'Trust in Organizational Authorities: The Influence of Motive Attributions on Willingness to Accept Decisions'. In Kramer and Tyler, *op. cit.*, 331–357.

15 Powell, W.W. (1996) 'Trust-Based Forms of Governance'; Burt, R.S. and M. Knez (1996) 'Trust and Third Party Gossip'. In Kramer and Tyler, *op. cit.*

16 Lester, R.K. (1998) *The Productive Edge: How Industries are Pointing the Way to a New Era of Economic Growth*. New York: W.W. Norton.

17 Gratton, L. (2000) *Living Strategy: Putting People at the Heart of Corporate Purpose*. London: Prentice Hall and the *Financial Times*.

18 Cumano, M.A. (1997) 'Microsoft Makes Large Teams Work Like Small Teams'. *Sloan Management Review* Fall: 20.

Trust as an Equity   2

TRUST IS A COMPETITIVE ASSET

Trust can become a new competitive asset in the firm. It may be thought of as a new invisible. Perhaps it is helpful to think of it as an internal equity yielding long-term return, based on the 'marketplace' of transactions and relationships within the firm. Like a conventional equity, trust is both uncertain and potentially volatile in the short run. Its value may be reduced by shifting confidence. It may lose value, or have its value temporarily suspended by management inconsistency and changed behaviour. The equity of trust may become more secure, given the development of confidence.

Information is crucial to trust. Trust implies risk. It is a gamble, a risky investment. Developing trust can be perplexing. There is usually less information available than required to make an accurate assessment of the potential success of a new relationship based on trust. The clues used to overcome a decision on trust do not eliminate risk; they simply reduce it. On the basis of reduced information, people become willing to take a risk because they have decided that the development of the relationship is sound. A change in goals can lead people to participate; the consistency of a campaign also can get people involved, but commitment is dependent on trust for making the relationship sustainable.

Trust gains value on the basis of consistency of performance, confidence and integrity. It becomes secure on the basis of reputation. Trust is not easily quantifiable, its unit of measurement being imprecise. It is difficult to unravel trust or low trust from their embedded position in a complex set of social relations. Calculating the value of trust requires clarification of terms and units. If not calculable in precise terms, together with many things of great importance in social organization, its value is verifiable as an asset.

Why invest in trust? At the very least, to try to overcome the negative cost of low trust and mistrust. The reduction in direct monitoring, and the need for widespread contribution to performance improvement as well as for employee information and knowledge, are all dependent on the development of trust. If 'people are our most important asset', to use an oft-quoted management cliché, the trust of people is of high value. Employees want to understand the contribution they can make; they want to be respected and valued for it. There is a search for revitalizing the dignity of work.

WHY LOYALTY IS NOT ENOUGH

All major firms are concerned about the retention of key people. They might well value loyalty as a critical asset. While loyalty is a useful quality, it may not be suited to today's competitive environment. These days corporate loyalty is much less significant than loyalty to a working team or a few close colleagues. Following the restructuring of the 1990s, many executives retreated into cautious individualism – focusing on just doing their jobs well. Loyalty became 'the enemy of change'. It is a fundamentally conservative instinct.[1] Perhaps the script for traditional loyalty of this kind needs to be rewritten. Loyalty can make people risk averse, simply because there is little extra reward for taking chances. Trust is more dynamic.

Loyalty-based management assists client retention – as employee loyalty grows, so does customer loyalty which creates value. 'Learning accumulates as people stay on the job.... by getting to know the customers, and providing the advantages knowledge gives. Long time hires add value to the company.'[2] Yet while it can be useful for building trust, loyalty is a contributory but not a sufficient component for building commitment to challenging new targets particularly demanding in today's new economy.

Loyalty may be pitted against change, particularly because it is traditionally associated with historic ties and structure. A stable relationship with familiar employees does not necessarily mean that customers will get the best service. This depends on something more. Loyalty is simply less dynamic, versatile or penetrating than a relationship based on trust.

Marks & Spencer was an excellent example of an organization built on employee loyalty and a job for life from the front line right up through the board. In the 1990s M&S tried to come to terms with the reality of the competitive situation on several fronts, following the complacency which was founded on success and smugness at the top levels of the organization. It had become a dinosaur, having jettisoned its flexibility, adaptability and dynamism following years of secure profits. Top management lost the capacity to generate new ideas or even to listen to their fashion experts.

In 1991 the board decided on a reduction of staff at headquarters – a restructuring which sent shudders throughout the organization because the purpose and extent of the redundancies were not explained to the staff. The traditional paternalistic relationship with staff was threatened. Trust was at a low ebb when people felt their 'job for life' with M&S was under threat (however unreal the threat was, since the stores were expanding at this time). On customer service M&S was outpaced by high street competitors. Good customer service is founded on people feeling good about themselves and the organization, which was hardly the case through much of the 1990s.

The design and presentation of merchandise was falling behind the competition, who were challenging M&S on style and price, since most of the clothing was produced in low-income Asian locations. Marks & Spencer clung onto its St Michael label of goods produced in the UK. The sourcing contracts to major UK suppliers had been the secret of its high quality and process efficiency throughout the 1970s and 1980s. But in the 1990s something else was needed and the board were slow to react to the competition, or to listen to the designers they hired. They thought in all their inward arrogance that they knew better what the customer wanted. The board were 'man and boy' M&S, and new ideas did not penetrate the arrogance. Poor performance led to the resignation of Richard Greenbury, the chairman and CEO, in 1998, and the appointment of Peter Salisbury for a brief period. Finally in 2000 the board was beginning to attract new people with a fresh look.

FORMS OF COLLABORATION

Like loyalty, there are a number of key concepts which are related to trust. We discuss the principal ones which particularly affect employee involvement and commitment. These observations are based on research. They are intended to clarify thinking:

- **Cooperation** is a temporary form of collaboration for a specific purpose – a separately negotiable act. An agreement to cooperate may be continued on the basis of habit, prior successful experience or trial and error. Cooperation can help build trust and trust can in turn strengthen cooperation.
- **Participation** may evolve from the instinct for cooperation, and is often related to the social nature of an organization. New management thinking may generate participation, but it will not be sustained on this basis alone. People are often willing to participate in a new initiative launched by management. They are willing to listen and offer to cooperate with what is requested.
- **Confidence** can arise once people begin to participate in a new initiative. It develops from consistency of feeling based on evidence. It is more tentative, less permanent than trust, and carries a lower risk. People can feel confidence in a particular line of policy, but they may continue to judge each new initiative on its merits.
- **Involvement** is based on the willingness to give of oneself in cognitive and emotional terms (head and heart). It builds continuity into separate instances of participation. Involvement relies on management consistency. People get involved in an improvement group because they are aware that their efforts on a previous occasion were taken seriously by management, or they have observed over time that the new initiative has become part of a consistent set of actions.

- **Commitment** may be achieved when cognitive and emotional involvement becomes intrinsic or persistently renewable. Commitment which is based on trust will be sustained, unless there is persistent evidence to contradict the basis of the new relationship. People become committed to performance-improvement efforts when management actions are consistent and reliable, and when their efforts are recognized, giving them a stake in the activity.

MUTUAL AND DISCRETIONARY TRUST

In the firm, we are concerned with two principal types of trust – mutual and discretionary. Mutual trust builds on the capacity of an organization to develop individual instances of inter-personal trust into a social phenomenon. Discretionary trust is based on the extent to which people are given scope and opportunity to organize the time or the quality and output of their work. Discretionary trust can be assessed by the measure of discretion and its time-span, refined by the progressive reduction in control mechanisms in the firm. It is a contributory factor to self-management. Discretionary trust may reinforce mutual trust. Mutual trust may develop alongside many different forms of discretionary trust.

Federal Express is a high-involvement, horizontally coordinated organization that encourages their employees to use their judgement above and beyond the rulebook.[3] FedEx employees are trusted to use their own judgement or use discretionary trust. It has helped make the company one of the highest-performing service organizations in the United States, and a great employer. The chief executive, Fredrick W. Smith, promotes front-line employees to feel secure in suggesting changes in workplace policy, questioning ill-advised management decisions. Within the company's Billing Center, for example, non-management employees are authorized to resolve customer billing problems up to $2000 credit or refund. Says Smith,

> There are lots of examples on a daily basis where our employee has the ability to satisfy a customer, but only at the risk of doing so either outside of policy, or where no policy exists. We want that employee to

satisfy the customer's need because they feel they have the authority or the power – the empowerment – to do whatever is necessary. The employee has to feel that he or she has the right, the authorization, or the backing to do whatever is necessary to satisfy the customer.[4]

In 1997 there was an all-out strike at Federal Express's principal rival, United Parcel Service. FedEx employees worked around the clock to deal with the additional volume of demand. At the end of this period, the company distributed $20 million as bonus payments to 90 000 operators in recognition of their efforts during the three-week strike. Fred Smith said that 'the last three weeks have been the best example in recent memory of why our 'People–Service–Profit' philosophy sets FedEx apart and why it is the cornerstone of our success.'[5]

Mutual trust in the firm is based on two forms of assessment – rational and emotional. Positive assessment of the rational components over time may have a direct and positive effect on the emotional basis of trust. Take as an example how an assessment of performance grows:

Assessment of discrete acts – 'What do I think of Beth's record on this?'
General appraisal – 'I believe that her positive approach will continue.'
Affirmation over time – 'Beth's record is pretty good. I hardly have to think of my assessment of her actions now. It seems to come naturally.'

The development of mutual trust takes place in three stages:

- An individual decision to award or withdraw (keep or break) trust.
  'I think I can trust my manager on this one'
- A transition through which decisions become generalized to relations in a particular social context.
  'We can count on management to deliver pretty regularly'
- The transition through which generalized trustworthiness and integrity are awarded to a group or organization, as trust becomes intrinsically associated with the collectivity or institution.
  'The reputation of management is excellent. We trust them'

Cognitive (rational)	Affective (emotional)
Assessment of	**Faith in**
Reliability	Care
Competence	Concern
Fairness	Openness
Consistency	Support

Figure 2.1 The basis of trust in the firm.

The first stage is based on individual assessment. The second is the generalization of this assessment on the basis of a series of repeated situations. The third is the changed state of mind in which a trusting outcome is assumed on the basis of this repeated assessment. Our research made it obvious that the second stage is the most difficult to achieve in the firm, the one which takes the longest to develop and is potentially the most vulnerable to reversal. The generalization from individual to significant group behaviour is of great importance. People are often very enthusiastic about participating in the quality programme. Sustaining participation is much more difficult (see Figure 2.1).

The initial willingness to participate with enthusiasm is based on a limited form of trust which requires further assessment. The perpetuation of collaborative behaviour by employees must necessarily be based on consistency and support. Trust is based first on an assessment of certain characteristics of behaviour on a rational basis. But the decision to trust or not to trust also relies on a form of emotional or affective appraisal of behaviour.

The durability of trust relationships is, above all, based on consistent behaviour over time. Trust is vulnerable to withdrawal because of inconsistent behaviour.

Aerco employees (Chapter 9) were asked to participate in performance-improvement teams for the first time and provide their suggestions. It was an experience radically different from the traditional command culture of this large defence contractor. People responded enthusiastically, but during this period, work teams and their supervision and remuneration were reviewed and radically changed without warning. Supervisors were briefed on the day the decision was implemented. There was no consultation and no discussion among managers about how to deal with a negative reaction. The initiative of the human resource director on behalf of senior management cut across the new collaborative opportunity. The management announcement was precipitous rather than prepared, largely out of fear of the consequences. Often it was found that giving bad news was held until the last possible opportunity – yielding the worst possible results. In an atmosphere of low trust, this only further compounded the problems.

In Aerco the lack of perceived fairness, openness and consistency had a devastating effect on the fragile trust which had been created – based on people's agreement to participate in performance-improvement teams. 'They [management] create barriers and want us to get on all the same with "that"' (gesture to a flip chart indicating a quality improvement problem-solving agenda). Aerco is a low trust firm. Its employee involvement programme failed to make any impact in 1994–5. It was a very costly exercise in terms of time.

BUILDING BLOCKS OF TRUST

Our research found that people will begin to develop trust in management on the basis of consistent, believable and frequent information about how the firm is doing in the competitive environment, and how local team or work group performance at the work level contributes to this. This builds a foundation for a better understanding of the performance of the firm. A management style based on openness is an important second component. Perceived fairness in work relations, and recognition of performance contribution, are equally significant to affirming trust. Trust will be built on the basis of competence, consistency and integrity, and be sustained as reputation.

> At Motorola, we enable people to do the things they want to do. Motorola provides the tools that give you the time and freedom to explore new worlds – that enable you to handle daily tasks in the most efficient way possible.[6]

The empowerment of people on the front line with rapid access to information encouraged customer retention and repeat buying at Motorola. Achieving major successes with quality improvement, Motorola encouraged employees to share ideas for improvement. Members of the Hi-Tech Team saved the company $250 000 by developing and implementing a strategy that increased production and reduced cycle time, without additional equipment or labour.[7]

There are several core components or building blocks of trust in the firm (Figure 2.2). These factors were identified repeatedly during observation and interview, and tested to a more limited extent in the quantitative survey.

Two types of information are important to the development of trust in the firm:

- **The disclosure or periodic provision of information** (macro information) about the competitive position and financial situation of the firm by management to the workforce, delivered in a timely and understandable manner.
- **The continuous provision of specific process and performance information** (micro information) to the people who work on the process, thereby awarding them more control over their work and generating the potential for 'ownership'.

- Information and communication
- Openness, fairness, and recognition which encourages employee 'voice'
- Reputation – based on competence, consistency and integrity

Figure 2.2 Building blocks of trust.

'Cascading' corporate information throughout the firm, customarily as part of a team brief, has become an important current feature of organizations. Our research showed that rarely is this practice anything more than a wooden, formalistic provision of information, which only a small proportion of the intended recipients can understand. To be effective, this type of information must be believable, understandable, timely and frequent. We found that information delivered locally by front-line managers, who had an understanding of the relationship of their own work to key corporate objectives, was the more successful means of communication. Employees were thus able to make the alignment of objectives real, were provided the key opportunity to make information valuable.

It can go badly wrong, however, if the information is untruthful or deliberately inaccurate. The following is a letter sent to the *Financial Times* in 2000 from New York:

> The problem seems to be that our senior management reach their positions by saying the right thing and playing internal politics rather than goal-focused delivery. This leads to a yes-man culture where senior management are never made aware of problems because the staff are too scared for their futures. This inhibits innovation and problem solution, with a direct impact felt on the bottom line and isolation of the board from the 'real world'.
>
> My current company has just made a substantial loss, is about to make thousands of staff redundant, and is being murdered in the marketplace by the opposition; staff morale is rock bottom. They have just published an article in the in-house newspaper saying that there is a 'tide of optimism' in the company. [8]

The provision of feedback information on the performance of a work unit – in a form which can be understood by all – may be a contribution to building discretionary trust. In ICL/Design to Distribution (D2D) fault information on printed circuit boards was customarily provided by production engineers in a language and format they found useful for reporting upwards. Once it was provided as a raw data printout to the local team in bare board production, many more process failures *could be* identified. It was delivered in a form they could understand.

DEVELOPING TRUST

Developing trust in an organization depends on a number of interrelated factors (see Figure 2.3):

- **Communication** is the first step to creating trust. Our research demonstrates that in successful firms messages based on new strategic intent were affirmed and communicated again and again. A new form of social contract began to develop on the basis of newly formed trust. There was confidence that management understood the strategic requirements of the new competitive situation and were consistent in their response. There was consistency in communicating the new messages to people about customers and competition.
- **Openness** is a leadership style which encourages people to be honest and forthright in the provision of information and the assessment of matters of importance. Many managers practise an open-door or open e-mail policy. Some walk about. But openness is more than just being available. It is a receptive cast of mind. It is based on familiarity through dialogue The Ashton site of D2D (Chapter 5) had a remarkably open environment based on frequent communication, providing candid information about the position of the firm, which was in a tough competitive situation. Managers were selected for their capacity to communicate and for their openness. No new engineering or technical staff were recruited without the capacity to communicate.
- **Fairness** is based on the perception that management will be as even-handed or equitable as possible. Procedural fairness can be defined as the lack of bias in procedures and roles. It is related to procedural justice. Interactional fairness can be defined as personal respect and status based on honesty, openness and goodwill. Fair process – fairness in the process of making executive decisions – is at the heart of building trust and unlocking ideas. A central idea emerging from recent research on fairness is that 'individuals are most likely to trust and cooperate freely in sharing their ideas when

Openness

Communication

Care and concern

Support and recognition

Fairness

Figure 2.3 Building trust: action points.

they feel recognised for their intellectual and emotional worth through what we call fair process'.[9]

'We find the work so much more challenging,' reported a team leader at the Ashton site: 'From our routine jobs, we have learned a lot of new skills on the basis of "sink or swim". The new supervisor is in the business of stretching us all. This gave us enormous confidence. If we couldn't do certain things, we were discreetly moved to other tasks, no reprimand, no feeling bad about it.'

- **Recognition** is based on the quest for respect, for acknowledgement of a job well done. To be effective, recognition is based less on contrived recognition schemes, publicized throughout the firm, than on the simple verbal or written acknowledgement.

- **Care and concern** are based on empathy for people and form the basis of progressive focusing on employee welfare and wellbeing.

EMPLOYEE VOICE

Once earned through these characteristics, trust can make it possible to enlist the voice of employees for the (often novel) provision of information, usually in the form of suggestions on performance or process improvement.[10] The provision of employee voice can be critical to performance improvement and potential innovation in the firm. We examined the stages of change and the consequences of change in an organization which encouraged the revaluation of specific local knowledge and expertise. We considered how employee information was valued as an input and how its continued provision was encouraged.

What are the stages of change, and the consequences of change, in an organization which encouraged employees to provide specific local knowledge and expertise? What promotes employee knowledge as a valued input to performance improvement, knowledge which has traditionally been seen as an important component of job control? The focus on process itself can be critical in releasing employee knowledge. Generation of an atmosphere where the employee voice is considered worth while and effective encourages the provision of employee knowledge.

Employee provision of local knowledge of the process in the workplace is usually based on tacit knowledge, which is the 'how' things are accomplished, or what has been learnt by doing. It is knowledge based on the experience of work and process rather than training or skill development. Tacit knowledge (of great significance to the process of innovation in technological development or scientific discovery) is a critical factor in understanding trust in the new relationships developed by process improvement. The contribution of tacit knowledge is becoming more widely recognized in process improvement in the workplace. The provision of tacit knowledge by the workforce is an important measuring rod of trust. The Japanese model of frequent incremental suggestions from each worker for the improvement of work processes is now familiar in European and American companies. By contrast, until recently, tacit knowledge was one of the key components of job control in the low trust environment of most Western firms. Tacit knowledge is considered in more detail in Chapter 4.

The measurement of trust in employee surveys is customarily based on the absence of fear. Alternatives include the components of discretionary trust and perception of management fairness. In our survey we used a well-established measurement of trust, but its explanatory components were too diverse to be of value. Most significantly, we found that trust related positively to recognition and a view that management had an interest in the welfare of its employees.

TRUST AND REPUTATION

Reputation

Trust is sustained by reputation. Reputation is assessed and reviewed by the observation of consistent behaviour over time. Once reputation is established, the necessity of testing the actions of trusted individuals becomes less and less important. Reputation has three components — competence, consistency and integrity (see Figure 2.4):

- **Competence** is earned reputation on the basis of knowledge, experience and ability. It is far easier for peers to assess competence on a continuous basis — be they fellow-employees or managers. Employees in the front line of organizations — at some distance from key management roles — rely on results or achievements to acknowledge competence.
- **Consistency** of initiatives is critical to the development of mutual trust. Consistency is far easier for the general working population to assess than competence and therefore is of cardinal significance for generating trust throughout the organization. It is the basis on which employees may be willing to consider the generalized form of trust in the organization.

In The Service Company (Chapter 6) the following comments were made by front-line managers responsible for implementing the new employee-involvement programme. They reflect acute problems of consistency in the management approach to new initiatives:

> If the commitment is not there from senior management, the programme will fail, and it will be seen by staff as just another 'flash in the pan.' *Handled right*, this could be the best thing to hit the company in the last 10–12 years.
>
> Most important is that the impetus for the programme is maintained by continuous backing from the top, without constantly introducing different and apparently contradictory policies.
>
> Similar schemes have been abandoned, which caused apathy.

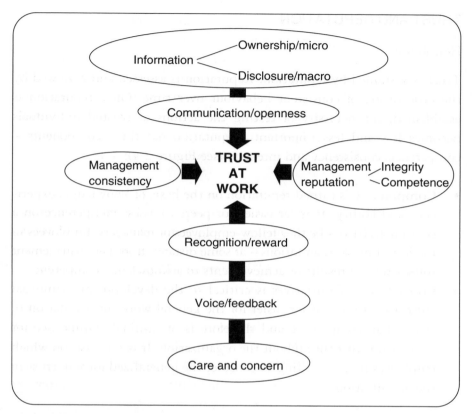

Figure 2.4 The components of trust in the firm

Employees in The Service Company gave the initiative a chance, but it lost momentum and focus because of further lack of consistency leading to multiple – seemingly unrelated – initiatives, and nearly annual restructuring throughout the 1990s. Despite the willingness of employees to identify with the improvement process initially therefore, the lasting outcome contributed to a lowering of management reputation. This inconsistency spilled over into adverse assessment of their competence and integrity as managers.

When there is sufficient consistency between new management thinking and behaviour, trust can develop and reputation can emerge. This seems to reflect a growing agreement on common objectives, overcoming the credibility gap. Building confidence is based on repeated expected behaviour, constant communication with few departures from this mode.

Consistency, or the perceived coherence of management initiatives and behaviour in the firm, often seem difficult to promote in a fast-changing environment. But firms which are continuously agile and responsive, changing radically and frequently to keep abreast of competition in product and strategy, can still be seen to be consistent to their people.

- **Integrity** may be defined as soundness of (moral) principle, rightness and honesty. It is based on the consistency and coherence of words and actions. The values and purpose of an organization provide the background on which integrity can be judged. An outer core of integrity addresses customers, the public and shareholders. The inner core is the consistent and cohesive approach to business experienced by those in the firm. This inner core is most significant for establishing trust.[11] Organizations like Hewlett-Packard had unusually consistent values and purpose, developed by their founders and expressed through many policies based on the HP Way. This could remain adaptable and unusually consistent over the years. Integrity means keeping promises and following through on commitments.

THE EXPANSION AND CONTRACTION OF TRUST

As a general rule, the expansion of trust is thought to generate increased scope for management action. The contraction of trust reduces the potential for such action. Employees may develop trusted relations with peers, technical collaborators such as engineers and selected managers, on the basis of reputation, while they still mistrust the organization in general and its management in particular. We found that the transition, from the award of trust on the basis of individual assessment to generalized or institution-based trust, is an exceedingly difficult one.

Two major propositions are critical to this transition:

- The form, frequency, relevance and credibility of communication in a large organization have a critical impact on the expansion and contraction of trust.

- Management consistency, reliability, and perceived fairness also have a critical impact on the capacity to generalize trust in the organization.

The potential terrain for the development of trust in the firm remains restricted for two reasons. Most structures are based on contract and accepted authority. Exit costs can be high. Restriction of interaction, familiarity, or the restricted opportunities to meet senior management challenge the prospect of building trust. They raise the problem of potential volatility, the perceived lapse of trust. Our evidence revealed that this was frequently so. Examples are found in the inconsistent initiatives, in The Service Company case, or seemingly thoughtless actions, bound to alienate employees, in Aerco.

Many firms, for example, adopted one or two initiatives which may begin to build trust, without changing other aspects of the organization. Employee involvement is often introduced, but makes little fundamental change in the way people are treated. We know that the culture of an organization cannot be altered by programmatic, often inconsistent, interventions which do not fundamentally alter values. They make little or no fundamental difference to the way people really think and make decisions.[12] Improving employee participation in performance improvement is at best a starting point. Trust implies risk and engenders a form of obligation. It raises new options. It may be generalized to social relations and organizations, so that we may identify high and low trust organizations. It is also possible to identify the factors contributing to resilience as well as fragility.

Thinking about trust as a competitive asset in the firm falls well short of explaining why people might consider it in their self-interest – short or long term – to be trusting at all. A simple answer may be the calculation that the competitive success or viability of the firm, and its high performance, are in the interests of all the people who work in the firm. As the traditional social contract founded on job security has been broken in the last ten years, fairness and recognition have become valued new assets as part of the quality of working life.

In logical terms, it still seems most difficult to understand the sacrifice of purely personal interest in favour of new relationships based on trust in the firm. Changing management thinking to revalue the contribution people can make throughout the firm may contrast sharply with low trust practices and inconsistent management initiatives. This has led to considerable cynicism on the part of employees. Low trust and adversarial industrial relations may be based on 'withholding moral involvement in employer's objectives, or working indifferently with little personal commitment, seeing the employer as pursuing his own objectives and feeling used'.[13]

The research on which this book is based indicated that employees seem willing to give their support to new performance improvement initiatives like quality. They seem willing to reconsider their conventional self-interest in favour of a new form of enlightened self-interest based on trust. They seem willing to forgo traditional job control for the provision of personal knowledge based on how processes function. Many examples provide evidence of a wish to be recognized, respected, valued for work and the contribution to improved performance.

REFERENCES

1 Heckscher, C. (1995) *White Collar Blues: Management Loyalties in an Age of Corporate Restructuring.* New York: Basic Books, 69.

2 Reicheld, F. (1996) *The Loyalty Effect.* Boston, MA: Harvard Business School Press.

3 Bowen, D.E. and E.E. Lawler III (1992) 'The Empowerment of Service Workers: What, Why, How and When'. *Sloan Management Review* Spring, 32.

4 AMA Management Briefing (1991) *Blueprints for Service Quality: The Federal Express Approach.* American Management Association Publications Division, 29–30.

5 'FedEx Rewards Employees for Dedication....' http://www.fedex/pr/employeebonus.html

6 Motorola website, http://www.mot.com/generalfacts.html

7 Weiland, R. (1994) 'Esprit de Corps'. *Successful Meetings* June.

8 Findlay, R. (2000) 'Crippled by the Inability to Listen', *Financial Times* 10 March.

9 Kim, W.C. and B.D. Henderson (1997) 'Fair Process: Managing the Knowledge Economy'. *Harvard Business Review* July–August.

10 The term is borrowed from A.O. Hirschman's 1970 classic, *Exit Voice and Loyalty*.

11 Shaw, R.B. (1997) *Trust in the Balance: Building Successful Organizations on Results, Integrity and Concern*. San Francisco, CA: Jossey-Bass.

12 Argyris, C. and D. Schon (1978) *Organisational Learning: A Theory of Action Perspective*. New York: Addison-Wesley; Schein, E. (1992) *Organisational Culture and Leadership*. San Francisco, CA: Jossey-Bass.

13 Fox, A. (1985) *Man Mismanagement*. London: Hutchinson, 74.

Releasing Energy: An Investment In Social Capital

3

RELATIONSHIPS

There is scarcely an activity which does not require collaboration —
running a fairground or designing a microchip. But what is the quality of
collaboration? Is it merely the interaction of people in groups who come
together and drift apart? Social capital is a term used to identify the value
of relationships which become significant enhancements to individual
actions. The willingness of people to create this form of capital is based
on their own assessment, not a formal organizational structure or a
campaign.

Social capital is a relatively simple concept for understanding the value
which relationships can generate. Social capital is more versatile than
concepts such as employee commitment, since it focuses attention on the
social value added which people are willing to build in a favourable
environment.

Silicon Valley is legendary for its lack of loyalty: turnover can be up to
50% per year, and companies seem more like temporary teams. One firm,
though, stands out in contrast to this trend: Hewlett-Packard. The
corporate objectives of HP are described as follows:

> The achievements of an organization are the result of the combined
> efforts of each individual in the organization working toward common
> objectives. These objectives should be realistic and should reflect the
> organization's basic character and personality.
>
> Relationships within the company depend on a spirit of cooperation
> among individuals and groups, a commitment to teamwork, and an

attitude of trust and understanding on the part of managers toward their people. These relationships will be good only if employees have faith in the motives and integrity of their peers, managers and the company itself. [1]

The HP Way was developed as soon as the organization was founded by Bill Hewlett and Dave Packard and was based on trust and respect for each individual who worked in the company. It was an open communication philosophy based on the practice of 'management by wandering about', and open doors to discuss feeling and frustrations in a constructive manner.[2]

Social capital, like that created at Hewlett-Packard, can reduce transaction costs, since individuals are no longer solely agents of value – contribution based on skill, effort and knowledge. Even in a low-wage environment such as Federal Express and Levi Strauss, employers have managed to get the best from their people with policies based on trust. Levi Strauss executives believe that 'by actively pushing responsibility, trust and recognition into the organization, we can harness and release the capabilities of all our people'.[3]

Social capital can be contrasted with the idea that individuals are necessarily influenced solely by the norms and values of the organization, leaving them little independent leverage on their actions. Employees have control over certain resources, and interest in the outcome of other resources and events. Social capital is based on willingness to collaborate not because of organizational requirements and management demand, but because of individual assessment. In a positive work environment, this assessment must be easier.

Social capital can facilitate action and help to achieve certain ends. Social capital is enhanced by trust. It becomes a valuable resource which can be promoted by trust. Trust is thus a contributor to social capital. Trust further expands the capacity for action based on social capital. Trust enhances the value of social capital. Management can invest in social capital by providing a context for it to grow and prosper. Social capital can become an additional resource – like trust, it is an invisible equity.

RADICAL CHANGES AT WORK

The nature of work has radically changed, driven not only by techno-logical change but also by increased global competition, requiring con-tinuous price reduction and reduced lead-time. Even computer-based systems of process control, contrary to earlier predictions of 'machine age Fordism', have required a more intelligent, flexible involvement of employees to make their work effective. Further, job complexity and the drive for higher and higher performance levels increases the need for involvement because of the difficulty of monitoring specialist work, and the cost of rehiring. Involvement without trust or involvement and with little employee voice will be tenuous at best.

The contraction of the manufacturing workforce, throughout the last decade, for example, has enhanced the scope for job redesign with shop-floor workers taking on basic planning, assessment, monitoring and maintenance responsibilities. It has also reduced supervisory and other control mechanisms, allowing employees more latitude in the organiza-tion of work and giving them more responsibility for the assessment of work performance. Many employees have taken over a wider range of jobs on a flexible basis, a transformation broadly unresisted by unions which have forgone traditional demarcation in favour of the preservation of members' jobs.

These important structural changes in the organization of work open up two new opportunities: first, a potential shift in employee outlook beyond the narrow confines of task and narrowly defined work location; second, an opportunity to consider employee contribution to the im-provement of processes by collaborating with colleagues outside the local work team. It is essential to try to understand in what circumstances it has been possible to develop social capital within the firm beyond the contractual basis of work, encouraging people to identify their own performance-improvement achievements with those of the firm.

Process improvement in the 1980s and 1990s (including lean pro-duction, total quality management, process re-engineering) demanded a drive for competitive performance and a powerful impetus for revaluing the employee contribution. The focus on process places a high value on collaboration. It gives new value to specific employee knowledge, particularly the tacit knowledge about how the process works in minute detail.

Employees were asked to provide detailed information and insight into potential process improvement. For many it was the first time they had been asked about their knowledge of key processes. Even in adversarial work environments, where job control had been the norm and retaining specialist knowledge from management the typical practice, this new form of recognition was a powerful force for motivating individuals and working groups to engage them in performance improvement.

Competition has driven the need for cost reduction, with the relaxation of direct monitoring and supervision of specialist work. Quality control, for example, with its armies of inspectors, has given way to schemes for employee assessment and certification of quality. Cost reduction has also reduced layers of supervision, making employees on the shopfloor responsible not only for monitoring and process control but also for basic maintenance.

Giving employees new responsibilities for local processes has a secondary impact on their willingness to invest more of themselves in improving performance. Often it took some time to get shopfloor employees the information in a form which they could understand. But once that information was available, the control and responsibility over the processes locally provided a limited form of empowerment, which further encouraged their cooperation.

Shortened product life cycles have put skill, training and employee motivation at a premium. Technological development in the work process has, contrary to what was expected, generated more complicated job roles rather than simplified, monotonous ones. People need to know more about process tolerances and related products; they need to be able to assess input supplies with more accuracy. They need to be more fully aware of marketing and customer service, monitoring and satisfaction. These changes have added to job functions more comprehensive tasks and responsibilities. Job flexibility offers the potential for enhanced interest in work and therefore motivation – the new variety of tasks being an improvement on monotony and repetition. In the new competitive environment, retaining people once they have been trained in a flexible work environment is of significant value. Rehiring is a considerable cost.

Although jobs were more interesting, more varied and with more responsibilities than before, people found that they were also being asked to work significantly harder to try to improve performance. Developing and maintaining employee commitment to the changed work circumstances required more than new forms of motivation promoted by initial recognition and limited empowerment. Building commitment over time was based on management consistency and a clear understanding of the contribution each employee made to competitive advantage – or an alignment of the firm's strategy with the activities of its front-line employees, and their awareness and acceptance of this.

'Unless every employee feels a deep sense of responsibility for firm success and has a clear channel for contribution, global leadership will remain elusive,' writes Gary Hamel.[4] In the next chapter, we discuss the alignment between employee effort and task and strategic goals of the firm. Rejuvenation of the mature firm also places high value on employee contribution – a mobilization of talent based on a common vision, formed by consensus. It can spread revitalisation to all departments. Coordination based on a collaboration which is diffused throughout the firm is essential to competitive success.[5] Collaboration of this kind indicates the high value of 'investing' in social capital.

MANAGING CHANGE WHILE NEGLECTING TRUST AND SOCIAL CAPITAL

Having identified the potential benefits of encouraging social capital, let us look at research findings which trace the consequences of neglecting trust and social capital. The views of employees in three large and prominent companies begin the story:

> My people feel devalued by all these management changes. They seem so foreign, and we are not consulted.

> I've worked for this company for a long time. Doesn't anyone care what I think should be done?
>
> The old strengths of our organization are being lost, like the dedication of people to their work and the informality of communication.

The first comment is basically asking for collaboration in the management of change – the right to be consulted. The second raises the significance and legitimacy of employee voice in the process of change and process improvement. The third recognizes that important values which can contribute to social capital had been lost or ignored. They demonstrate how people can feel devalued by change. They indicate how much local knowledge and potential for involvement can be sacrificed by large-scale radical change which takes little notice of the employee perspective.

Such reactions help to explain the difficulties of creating a suitable environment in which social capital can develop. They offer explanations for employee reluctance to collaborate with the change. In the decade between 1985 and 1995, employee attitude surveys in British industry revealed that morale was at an all-time low in major institutions, largely because of downsizing and the alteration of the traditional moral contact of employment. Yet this was precisely the time when companies began to embark on restructuring and rapid change, to meet the rigours of the recession and the downturn in business which had caused the downsizing in the first place. Companies which embark on change while remaining at the same site, in the same business and with the same workforce are usually regarded as the most difficult to change. But this, after all, accounts for rather a large company population in most economies.

Beginning to initiate change, and gaining acceptance, can be very difficult. Many companies in the rush to change have succeeded in cutting across both strongly held corporate values and people's feelings, often with scant reference to their existence. This carries a high risk. Change which goes this route can generate low trust, just at a time when they can prove particularly costly. To jettison the past (good and bad) is to invite resistance, or risk a form of 'opt out'. Such a rejection of the past devalues people, and what they have come to believe and respect. It can severely jeopardize the change effort.

The pace of corporate change, based on frequent restructuring and a multiplicity of successive management strategies introduced, promoted and discarded in many firms in the 1990s have seriously eroded management credibility. To many employees it may look like a 'slash and burn' approach to change, not a move with which they can identify. In many instances, it was accompanied by poor communication or very little effective communication at all. In Aerco a supervisor observed:

> The attitude of senior management towards employees is not all it should be. We are intelligent enough to realize that massive changes are imminent, but facts are being withheld and things which will have a lasting effect on the future are being glossed over.

Poor communication, together with the formidable consistency of the traditional culture, can build up resistance which becomes a powerful negative influence in the formative years. Both will provide a major obstacle to change. Openness and constant communication are the key to successful change. But communicate what? Some argue facts, not values. And how? Face to face, walking the job, not in videos, newsletters and large meetings.[6]

The language of change can become a serious barrier, focusing on a key set of new concepts which may not be developed or related to the existing culture, or newly presented concepts which are already embedded in values in one form or another, but presented as the newest fashion. New ideas (or seemingly new ones) used as ubiquitous slogans, or displayed as reminders throughout the workplace, will generate cynicism for new management jargon. These have been referred to as 'corporate graffiti'. Many change strategies are perceived by the workforce to be foreign, that is, foreign to the enterprise and 'the way things have always been done', or 'not invented here and therefore not for us'. Wherever the ideas originate, they obviously are poised so tentatively on the prevailing culture that their lack of integration is keenly felt by those on the receiving end.

These combined elements generate both a devalued view of management and inevitably a devaluation of people, just at a time when successful change may only be achieved with an employee-centred strategy. The process of change can, conversely, make employee stakeholders feel that they are the least important of all, and many explicitly say this. The attempt to engage employees in the change process, yet not view it as also applicable to management, can have very damaging effects, as it did in The Service Company.

Special meetings between management and five shopfloor engineers were initiated in an attempt to learn first-hand about their problems and suggestions. The first two meetings were very confrontational, and very little was accomplished. By the third monthly meeting, the atmosphere began to change, and representatives were encouraged to identify problems with colleagues and bring them to the next meeting. The experience turned in the fourth and fifth meetings, when the engineers began to identify with management, by acknowledging the difficulties of taking up their own suggestions for either financial or technical reasons.

Management at The Service Company suspended the meetings after this, believing them to be of limited usefulness. It is likely that any meeting of this kind would meet a similar fate elsewhere in the company. Consultation is an ineffective technique where perceptions of the job and attitudes to work remain unchanged. It is equally ineffective where they begin to change and become a potential source of social capital, yet this goes unrecognized for its potential significance.

Successful change, built on strong leadership, drive and effective communication may draw on a number of elements from the existing corporate culture to be incorporated into new corporate values, thus maintaining continuity. The existing culture will dilute very slowly in any case, so why not seek the advantage of building bridges with the past, thereby facilitating change? Building bridges to the past can have very practical payoffs. If there is scope for collaboration and building social capital, extra effort to tap into the past can yield results.

Until it launched its major change programme in 1987, Shorts Aviation, the aircraft manufacturer (part of the Canadian Bombardier Group), had been a traditionally organized aircraft manufacturer with high government subsidies. Their change programme, which is driven by quality performance, has generated new employee-led teams in more than half of their improvement programme. Quality workshops incorporated employee local knowledge, sometimes spanning generations. A technique of metal spinning, which had been lost for a generation in favour of a quicker and cheaper welding method, was reintroduced. Knowledge of the technique was brought back by the son of a previous Shorts employee, who had long since retired. The old technique, a quality approach to the job, reduced material and labour costs, lead-times, inspection and rework, involving a considerable savings on the manufacture of jet engine pods.

Changing job design and reward systems to fit employee aspirations and corporate strategy can begin the attempt to make people feel valued, encourage them to make suggestions about processes and services and take initiatives. These can encourage innovation. Somewhere along this route, traditional cultural values will begin to change when people feel that they are a part of the new process, and may then even begin to identify with it.

An engineering works team in The Service Company in 1992 completed surveys of a kind done throughout the company on internal services impinging on the team's work. The evidence from colleagues (who had never previously been asked for such specific findings on the organization of their own work) was received with great interest by the team. In the presentation, many additional points were made, illustrating the scope of local knowledge, high job involvement, and a keen sense of both quality and customer service. Reflecting on this afterwards, their young manager indicated how swift the change had been: 'A year ago if I had handed out a questionnaire, I would have been told, "On yer bike!" Things have really changed.'

The British workforce is often criticized for poor workmanship, low productivity and lack of responsibility. Considering the structure and organization of work as well as low levels of training (compared with other European Union members or the USA and Canada) and the capability and outlook of management, it is not altogether surprising that change is difficult to achieve.

Cynicism and fatalism often prevail in the work environment. Yet the British have no monopoly on cynicism, as often thought with some twisted pride. In the United States, cynicism in the workforce, which is based primarily on unrealized expectations of 'the American dream',[7] seems both more penetrating and long lasting. In Britain, cynicism remains largely at enterprise level, and is therefore curable at enterprise level, if there is a will to do so.

There is overwhelming evidence from the research that employees wish to be involved in change, provided their involvement is considered meaningful, based on respect for their contribution and results driven, not just an exercise in 'energizing' the workforce.

CREATING SOCIAL CAPITAL: INVOLVING PEOPLE IN PERFORMANCE IMPROVEMENT

Performance-improvement initiatives such as quality management and process re-engineering were introduced in many firms from 1985 to 1995. Most were based on training programmes, tools and techniques which failed to be sustained or embedded in the organization. There are exceptions, of course, among highly successful competitive firms. But for the most part these initiatives were 'bolted on', lacking impact on the organizations, which failed to make any significant changes in the way they operated or the way in which employees could relate to new competitive goals. It could be argued that these initiatives failed to create an environment to encourage the development of social capital in relation to the changes they were trying to promote.

The principal reasons for the failure of these performance-improvement efforts were poor organizational learning and internal mistrust. Organizations which fail to meet the challenge of changed competitive circumstances generally have poor communication and low levels of employee motivation and a low regard for entrepreneurship, all of which prevent performance-improvement initiatives like quality from taking hold. We need to address the problem, 'What does or does not encourage employees to identify with performance improvement as a shared corporate goal?'

The development of performance improvement based on quality can test the prospects for building social capital based on new relationships in the firm. In the early decades of the twentieth century European and American manufacturers maintained high-quality performance by relying on pride in craft from skilled workers, and introduced quality control for unskilled labour, materials and equipment. Continuous inspection of production and work performance had a triple purpose: (1) not letting defective products into the market, (2) tracing equipment and processes with a view to correction and (3) providing feedback sanctions on workers who produced defective work. This led to the establishment of quality control departments which were organizationally separate from line management. They introduced a form of institutionalized distrust.

External inspection of this kind was costly, and total assurance of quality ran the risk of pricing products out of the market. 'Trade-offs' were made to achieve a product which was acceptable in the market at a given price by minimizing the cost of testing and inspection. Japanese manufacturers demonstrated that the calculation of these trade-offs, which had become the science of quality control, can be drastically altered by achieving much higher quality at low-quality assurance costs.

New concepts of quality, which became popular in the 1950s, were based on the prevention of defects by continuous improvement. It was found that defects in workmanship could be reduced if employees were given skills and equipment to monitor their own work. It could be made even more effective if they were given responsibility for ensuring quality output, and trusted in this exercise by the removal of external inspection.

Is there anything intrinsic to performance improvement which offers a new terrain for the consideration of trust in the firm? The emphasis on participation in the process is among the key things which make a difference. The focus on measurement and continuous improvement in quality performance puts a premium on creating transparency in processes and enhances the value of information collected in the micro processes. This raises the value of information from people on the front line. Their voice becomes a more valuable one. It raises the prospect of adding value to the employee role and valuing social capital.

Successful quality management, and its sustained practice over a long period of time, require much more than technical or statistical analysis, measurement and monitoring. Quality output does require excellent equipment and a good skill base, but it also depends on new concepts of management, communication, and broad-based staff involvement. Few other current concepts of change in business were so demanding of constancy, and so dependent on a change in the traditional relationships in the firm. Quality output was driven by local necessity and the specificity of performance improvement rather than a change in management ideology. This required the effort to build involvement in quality and gave significance for involvement in subsequent programmes. Quality circles became the first important means of generating employee involvement. But these failed, often despite local enthusiasm, to fulfil their anticipated promise, because of lack of organizational support, isolation from mainstream activities, lack of persistence or poor programming.

Involving employees in improving quality performance included:

- Participation in quality-awareness training, learning basic tools and techniques
- Participation in new organizational forms and activities, such as cross-functional or problem-solving teams
- The use of new instruments for process improvement

All of these imply new forms of learning, new tasks, and a focus on process. In general, people in our sample were enthusiastic about their quality training. For some it was the first non-skill-based training and corporate awareness with which they had been acquainted. Most of the employees who participated in our survey were reluctant to believe that quality awareness and training would be implemented throughout the firm. In most cases they were correct.

These employees hoped that their contribution would be valued, and that they would be recognized for it. Openness, fairness and recognition were factors which could confirm trust and help make it more secure. To be sustained, we found that the alignment of initiatives and the consistency and credibility of the management message were essential. Among the firms collaborating with the research we found the defining characteristics of both high and low trust firms, and were able to identify the elements of each. We found firms in which management credibility was reduced in the workforce by introducing too many initiatives at once. We found firms in had managed to develop fragile and tentative trust by getting people to contribute their knowledge and effort to performance improvement for the first time. This led us to consider the development and durability of trust and its vulnerability.

The constancy of performance, based on precise and continuous quality assessment, requires the widest involvement in the improvement and monitoring of all local processes. The cost would be prohibitively high if driven by professionals. High job involvement was obvious among employees surveyed which made people, not surprisingly, identify with quality. As a shop steward in Aerco said in a team meeting: 'I am quality!'

Employees are expected to develop new competencies – for assessing and reporting process measurement. Individual employees reacted with enthusiasm to gaining additional training and responsibility on the basis that it would make their jobs more secure. They are customarily asked to provide suggestions on quality improvement individually to a manager, in a team discussion, or in a site- or corporate-wide suggestion scheme.

When quality improvement programmes were not accompanied by effective leadership on the front line, or were not supported in organizational terms, the result was a loss of faith in management consistency and sense of purpose. It frequently generated disappointment after initial enthusiasm.

Employee involvement in quality drew attention to the prospects for new forms of organizational learning. To be successful, employee involvement required two forms of alignment: the alignment of the quality programmes with other changes in the organization, and the alignment of people's perceptions of their contribution to improved performance with the competitive goals of the firm. Few business concepts were as demanding of constancy of performance as TQM, and therefore as dependent on learning and alignment. These cannot be achieved without change, based on effective leadership and constant communication.

Quality management encouraged a strong institutional structure based on learning and encouraging innovation. Thinking about the promise of the quality moment, and its presumed failure, a recent author has written 'total quality is no more than a label for practices that organizations were going though anyway . . . [or] fundamentally a way of using language and ideas to mobilize actions that are often talked about, but not frequently actioned.'[8]

While quality management was felt to have opened up the organization to new ways of thinking, some scholars obviously felt that this was not enough. Ed Lawler, who has written about high-performance teams and other forms of employee participation, recognized that quality schemes which demand organizational redesign called for moving substantial amounts of information, knowledge and power downwards, which could in the short run be satisfying. But he felt that this would not generate economically effective performance, unless long-term equity and motivation problems could be rectified by moving rewards downwards.[9] Most quality management programmes, including those with considerable emphasis on employee involvement, had neither new reward structures nor did they consider developing a new moral contract based on employability. All but two of the collaborating firms were restructuring and developing other change initiatives at the same time as introducing quality management in the mid-1990s. But there was little enough obvious consideration of a new employee contract or a concerted attempt to decentralize responsibility or alter reward based on performance. The survey to follow therefore offers an opportunity to consider what an employee would value in return for involvement without radical changes in the employment contract.

BUILDING AWARENESS – NEGLECTING TRUST

Survey research results

The research started with the basic idea that quality output required excellent equipment and a good skill base, but was probably dependent for its success on new concepts of management, communication, sustained commitment and broad-based staff involvement. We hoped that by examining the potential contribution of employee involvement to quality performance we would be better able to understand a potential shift from the contractual neutrality of work to a new relationship between employee and manager, a new basis for building social capital.

Recognizing that the end of job security in most firms had broken what was a traditional employment contract, we were interested to explore on what basis a new relationship could be developed between employees and management. To put it another way, what makes people wish to participate, and subsequently get involved in performance improvement? Why do they stay involved and possibly get committed? And how can this be perpetuated?

The case study chapters of this book (Chapters 5–10) and much of the empirical support for the case material are based on findings from a research with six major firms from 1992 to 1995. All the firms had well-established quality improvement programmes. The research was based on the assumption that employee commitment to quality was required to build and sustain high-quality performance. Research was both qualitative, generating comprehensive case studies for each of the firms, and quantitative, based on a major survey of employee attitudes on the firm and on the performance-improvement initiative on quality.

During months of observation of team activity and work processes, complemented by personal and group interviews in each of the firms, it became obvious that there was a factor of considerable importance, which had been ignored prior to going to the field. This was the concept of trust and its potential role in the firm. Information and communication were vital to understanding the generation of trust. People seemed initially reluctant to commit themselves to new performance-improvement initiatives for TQM unless they had a fairly clear and comprehensive understanding of their role in the new initiative, and how it related to the current strategy of the firm.

Summary findings of the research are

- Front-line people believed themselves to be relatively well informed about quality and the company's competitive position.

- But their views on commitment to the organization or work team, and perceived fairness and recognition in the organization, tended to detract from their willingness to identify their own performance with improved quality performance.

Thus people understood in cognitive terms what was required on the basis of information provided, but their relationship to the organization failed to encourage them to be motivated to do anything more than what was required.

Survey population

The survey, conducted from January to March 1994, gave us a rare opportunity to observe in a systematic manner the introduction of six quality programmes in different stages of development (from recently initiated to mature) in different organizations.

More than one thousand employees in five of the six collaborating firms returned the postal questionnaire (consisting of eighty questions on a one-to-five scale from strongly agree to strongly disagree). Nearly half of them were working as direct production operators; the others were in test and inspection, or installation and maintenance engineers. 54% were skilled; 73% were male.

The population had a strong longevity of service – more than 80% had been with the same firms for more than six years; 63% had been more than 11 years with the company. Asked about their intention to stay with the company, 62% said that they wanted to stay with the company for at least five years longer, or until retirement.

All the firms except one had initiated redundancy programmes following the recession from 1990 to 1992. After this period of contraction, one firm was hiring again three years later, using temporary contracts only. While redundancy programmes have an immediate impact on employee perceptions of the firm, they were not found to be the single most important influence on employee attitudes toward the firm and their behaviour. Confidence in senior management and the perceived consistency of their own initiatives (to keep the firm competitive) were much more significant. Communication was critical: one firm valued communication on a constant basis, and were able to maintain motivation despite continual employment uncertainty; in another, a firm in which the security of employment was not an issue, management failure to maintain communication had a serious impact on employee morale.

Initiating and implementing quality

All participating companies had established quality programmes between 1985 and 1993. About one quarter of the sample had been working on quality for up to one year. About one third had been working on quality for one to three years and another third for more than three years.

There was thus a high level of quality awareness and its perceived importance in all firms: 85% of respondents believed that the company had quality as a priority. There was also a high level of participation in quality: 83% of respondents had participated in quality improvement activities in their work group. Combined with relatively high levels of a recognition of the importance of quality and its impact on individual performance, it seemed obvious at least that the introduction of quality and the provision of information had been successfully accomplished by most firms.

The implementation of quality measures for employees of all firms in the sample was perceived to be much less successful than high levels of quality awareness. Only about 50% felt that quality activities had made them see their performance differently. While 80% demonstrated an awareness of quality, less than half (47%) were using quality techniques on a regular basis (daily or several times per week) and only just over half only (54%) felt that quality was implemented effectively.

Part of the problem was found in the need for more frequent and effective performance feedback. About 70% of the employees surveyed were aware of improvement needs, and the importance of quality. And about the same proportion felt that continuous improvement helped people to solve problems themselves. But the impact was reduced by lack of systematic implementation in order to gain from these positive observations.

Three principal reasons emerged to explain the high awareness of quality and its lack of success in implementation:

- Poor leadership on the front line
- Short-term production drives which took precedence over quality improvement
- A pronounced blame culture based on low trust.

TRUST – THE MISSING FACTOR

The summary of results in Table 3.1 indicates the decline in positive responses to the questions – beginning with a high rating on understanding of the challenges facing the company, and the lowest on whether management can be counted to give employees 'a fair deal.' The questions are grouped in common headings, beginning with 'being informed', which illustrates strong support for an appreciation of what is required. Employees in the survey felt that they understood the competitive position of their firms very well (92%) and 82% felt that company profitability was of importance to them. Respondents were in search of more information on how well the firm was doing in its own sector (74%).

Whatever the company performance, or its experience with quality management, employees agreed that these factors were of similar importance. Thus people in ICL, which was a high-performing firm experienced in quality management, and Aerco, which was not, responded similarly to understanding the competitive challenge, relating their own performance to company performance and indicating that they wished to have more information.

The delivery of information – on the basis of team briefs – was considered to be effective by just over half (56%), which may explain the significance of the local rumour mill as an alternative way of obtaining information.

The willingness to make an effort on behalf of the organization was

Table 3.1 Trust – the missing factor

	% answering yes
Becoming informed	
I understand the competitive challenges facing my company	92
The profitability of the company is important to me	82
I would like more information on how well we are doing in the industry	74
Team briefs or meetings regularly provide me with useful information	56
Rumour is the more reliable way of getting information round here	43
Effort on behalf of the organization	
To know that my work has contributed to the organization pleases me	85
My effort is also an organizational effort	77
I am willing to put myself out to help the organization	68
Voice	
If you have a good idea it will be heard	59
The suggestions I make can affect company performance	56
Managers encourage us to give our opinions	50
Relating to the firm	
I am proud to tell people whom I work for	47
I feel myself to be part of the company	44
I would recommend someone to join the company	44
Trust 1	
I can disagree with my manager without fear of being criticized	46
People are more criticized than praised	55
People I work with are reluctant to speak their minds	53
Trust 2	
Most people who work with me show loyalty to the company	40
Most people I work with feel valued by the company	13
Top management have a sincere interest in the welfare of their employees	9
Management can be counted on to give us a fair deal	8

very high, which ought to be contrasted with the perceived relationship to the firm. The willingness to make an effort on behalf of the organization is reflected in high job involvement. This strong affirmation of willingness to make an effort is mitigated by how people feel about the organization, indicated by feeling part of the company, proud to work for it, willing to recommend people to the company, as is obvious from the answers in the first of the trust group of questions.

About half the sample supported the importance of employee voice. Three factors were very closely related on whether or not employees were willing to provide suggestions about performance improvement:

- If you have a good idea, it will be heard.
- My suggestions can affect company performance.
- Managers encourage us to give our opinions.

The questions which assessed the perceived atmosphere of trust and fairness had less promising results

- I can disagree with my manager without fear of criticism – 46%
- The suggestions I make are considered fairly – 39%

There were two key questions on trust.

- People are more criticised than praised – 55%
- People are reluctant to speak their minds – 53%

Forty per cent of respondents felt loyalty towards the company. The performance of the firm on quality management had little impact on these key trust indicators, which were more closely related to the culture and working environment.

The second group of trust questions – about feeling valued by the firm and whether or not management has a serious interest in the welfare of employees – was exceedingly low, indicating a strong current of low trust in the relationship of employees to the firm across the whole sample. Based on fairness, these questions convey a strong 'them and us' perception by the employees in the sample, regardless of the success of employee-involvement programmes. Perceived fairness across the sample companies is very low:

- People feel valued by the company – 13%
- Top management have a sincere interest in employees – 9%
- Management can be counted on to give us a fair deal – 8%

It is these findings in particular which prevent companies from realizing the full potential of the workforce, or the quality programmes in which they seek to involve them.

MANAGEMENT SUPPORT

One of the major problems affecting the implementation of quality was the perceived lack of management support:

- Nearly 50% of the respondents felt that senior management talked a lot about quality, but did little.
- 67% felt that senior management only cared about output.
- 40% felt that this was because they were working on too many initiatives at once.
- 65% believed that supervisors gave strong support to quality.

Management consistency also has a strong impact on building trust.

JOB INVOLVEMENT, TEAM INVOLVEMENT

People in the sample showed a high rate of job involvement:

- 85% felt satisfaction with a job well done.
- Nearly 75% of people believed that their feelings were affected by how well they did the job, and associated a good opinion of themselves with how well the job was done.
- A staggering 91% were interested in having additional training, reflecting a low level of training on the front line of UK manufacturing compared to other EU countries or the USA.

While a very high proportion of people (89%) worked in teams, and a majority expressed a wish to have more feedback on team performance on a regular basis (60%), 63% felt that their own achievement was the same as their work team achievement. While people were willing to put themselves out for the team and keen to know that personal effort made a contribution to the team, this seemed to be based more on loyalty than on an association between personal and team performance. This is not surprising, since performance was not measured or rewarded on the basis of the team.

ORGANIZATION AND TEAM COMMITMENT

While employees seemed willing to be responsive to the needs of the organization, they neither identified with it not felt committed to it. It has already been demonstrated that people did not recognize fairness, nor did they think management took an interest in, or cared about, them.

Front-line management (supervisors, first level of management) were considered in transition to more effective leadership roles in quality:

- 65% believed that front-line management were committed to quality.
- 57% that they were helpful and supportive.
- 52% that they were good leaders.

Based on observations made in the course of initial qualitative research, we felt that team commitment would be stronger and more significant than the traditional form of organizational commitment, based on company, division or site. We assumed that employee loyalty and, more important the willingness to commit themselves, were probably stronger for the team than the organization itself (see Table 3.2).

We made this observation, even though we have previously noted that people tend to assess their performance on an individual rather than a team basis. Performance measurement is based on individual motivation for the job. Commitment is stronger to the team than the organization. This has considerable implications for the now popular redesign of organizations in favour of product- or customer-based teams. On team commitment:

- 85% were willing to put themselves out for the team.
- 81% were willing to help make the team successful.

Table 3.2 What makes employees work best?

What do employees seem to be looking for when asked to provide higher levels of quality performance? The following list was drawn up by a design team of frontline employees in the components business of Aerco. It is a useful list against which to consider current company performance and potential improvement.

The findings can be summarized as the intrinsic interest in, and value of, work fostering job involvement, the social capital built from relationships and the powerful part that recognition can play in motivating people. The exercise began with the statement,

We believe Aerco people work best when......

Quality of work, personal challenge
- we have **meaningful work**, because we feel valued.
- work offers us **a challenge**; we can see our achievements
- we have **variety** in our work
- we can see the finished product and **take pride** in it
- we have **good training** to gain confidence

Trust and social capital
- we **trust** our fellow workers
- we are part of a **team**
- we have **collective goals** and objectives
- the **leaders** are part of the team and **share its values**

Recognition
- we are **recognized for doing a good job**
- **success is communicated** as well as failure

Alignment
- our **tasks are clearly defined**
- we are **involved in and understand change**
- managers and supervisors **understand our work**
- we **understand where we fit** in the organization
- we **share in the success of the company**.

- 78% said they really cared what happened to the team.
- 74% felt a strong loyalty to the team.
- 63% said that they felt that their own achievement was the same as that of the team.

EMPLOYEE PERCEPTION AND EFFORT

The quantitative results offer an opportunity to consider the relevance of building social capital in the context of employee involvement in performance improvement. We found that although an understanding of the new programmes and tasks at hand seemed to be well established, the emotional or affective side of trust – or feeling appreciated by and relating to the firm – were very weak across the sample of employees. This must have been a serious draw on the potential energy of people in all firms.

Strong relationships to the local work team, rather than the firm as a whole, indicate a potential arena for strengthening social capital. This is based primarily on loyalty and sociability, creating ties which are more than simply vocational. The qualitative research in the case study chapters will indicate the difficulties of sustaining the work of process or cross-functional based teams without these ties of loyalty and sociability. In order to benefit from new forms of social capital in the firm, the perceived working environment requires a move to greater recognition of specific acts, valuing employees in general terms on a consistent basis.

The advantages of promoting an environment which can support greater social capital can pay significant rewards in terms of employee willingness to give more of themselves. The quantitative research indicates that globally this had not yet been developed in the firms surveyed.

The following major propositions emerge from our research:

- Employees may be enthusiastic about initial participation and willing at least to consider the new opportunity of becoming involved in performance improvement.
- Quality programmes can provide an interesting opportunity to change employee perceptions.
- The willingness of people to participate is affected by the climate of trust in the firm. If people do not feel valued by the organization, trust is low and the 'us and them' remains strong, this will affect their willingness to participate over time.
- Employee involvement in quality will remain programmatic, or a 'bolt-on' to the organization, if there is a poor employee identification with the effort.
- If people are unsure of the relationship of their contribution to strategic goals, this will affect their willingness to continue to participate.

- Employee involvement will only become embedded in the organization when people feel valued for the contribution they make, and understand their role and their contribution to competitive performance – in summary, that there is recognition for their efforts and the relationship of their efforts to strategic goals is aligned.

REFERENCES

1 Corporate objectives of Hewlett-Packard, http://www.hp.com/abouthep/corpobj.html (30/12/97).

2 The HP Way, http://www/hp/abouthp/hpway.html (30/12/97).

3 'Responsible Commercial Success'. All About Levi Strauss&Co, http://www.levistrauss.com/lsc_mission.html

4 Hamel, G. (1994) *Competing for the Future*. Boston, MA: Harvard Business School Press, 136–137.

5 Ghoshal, S. and C. Bartlett (1996) 'Rebuilding Behavioural Context: A Blueprint for Corporate Renewal'. *Sloan Management Review* 37: No. 2, Winter; Baden Powell, C. and J. Stopford (1992) *Rejuvenating the Mature Business*. London: Routledge; Beer, M., R. Eisenstadt and B. Spector (1990) *The Critical Path to Corporate Renewal*. Boston, MA: Harvard Business School Press.

6 Larkin, T.J. and S. Larkin (1996) 'Reaching and Changing Frontline Employees'. *Harvard Business Review* 14: No. 3.

7 Kanter, D.L. and P.H. Mirris (1989) *The Cynical Americans: Living and Working in an Age of Discontent and Disillusion*. San Francisco, CA: Jossey-Bass.

8 Pfeiffer, J. (1994). *Competitative Advantage Through People*. Boston, MA: Harvard Business School Press, 206-207.

9 Lawler, E. (1992) *The Ultimate Advantage: Creating the High Involvement Organization*. San Francisco, CA: Jossey-Bass, 57.

Releasing Value: An Investment in Learning and Alignment

4

THE RELEVANCE OF ORGANIZATIONAL LEARNING

How well an organization adapts and innovates in an unpredictable environment is a measure of its learning capability. Organizational learning is a term which allows us to understand the difference between one-off programmes which fail to take root and others which become part of the way things are done. This distinction is reflected in two types of organizational learning – that which involves piecemeal adaptation, and that which contributes to significant organizational transformation. These two types of learning are particularly useful for thinking about performance improvement initiatives. They allow one to see the distinction between one-off attempts to rectify practices and the significant changes in values and behaviour which make performance initiatives part of the organization's structure and culture.

Most of the research and writing on organizational learning has been based on modelling the activities of senior management.[1] But rapid and frequent changes in competition require a response based on the learning capacity of all employees throughout the firm. A measure of success is the capacity of the firm to implement these changes as widely as possible. The growth of technological complexity places a higher value on diffused learning in all functions, and on the openness and collaboration of cross-grade, cross-functional cooperation.

The focus on process in performance improvement questions traditional relationships in the firm, and offers an opportunity to consider new forms of interaction. It simplifies and concentrates new forms of action. In

Table 4.1 Types of learning

Programmatic	Organizational
Reactive	Proactive
Adjustment	Turnover
Adaptive	Assumption
Operational	Policy
Mechanistic	Evolutionary
Adaptive	Generative

focusing attention end to end, the product or service becomes the key element. Work becomes revalued as a contribution to the improved process; it requires communication.

Most organizations use programmes like TQM to detect errors which they can correct in performance, while maintaining the central features of the organization intact. A second stage of learning only takes place when new knowledge is translated into new forms of behaviour which are replicable.[2] Two forms of learning have been contrasted: programmatic and organizational (Table 4.1).

In much of the programmatic learning or 'bolt-on' activities typified by TQM, organizational defensive mechanisms thwart the change from developing because they are too prescribed, giving people little opportunity to reconsider the way they think. If learning is not developed, the initiative will fail to challenge existing organizational norms and resolve conflicts between them.[3]

TACIT KNOWLEDGE AND ORGANIZATIONAL LEARNING

To make learning significant for employees, by giving them a framework to understand the relationship between their activities and the corporate goals of the firm, *alignment* is essential. A focus on *process*, rather than structure or product, begins to value the employee contribution in a way which recognizes local expertise (often for the first time). The prospect of creating a new relationship between employee and manager, based on a mutuality of interests, may generate a new form of *trust*. The contribution of employee *tacit knowledge* to performance improvement may be generated by the willingness of employees to identify with new corporate goals and take them on as their own.

Tacit knowledge, customarily used in connection with innovation in an organization – particularly technological innovation – may be defined as *the implicit, procedural, uncodified and embodied knowledge included in how people became familiar with work*. This is distinct from skills and technical knowledge which can be taught and reproduced through training. In an adversarial work environment, tacit knowledge has always been a valuable source of job control by employees, who thereby ensured their indispensability to a working process. Improvement of the processes on which quality management is based places a new and high value on this type of knowledge. To put it another way, to be able to tap into tacit knowledge may be a potential source of continuous innovation in an organization. That employees are willing to provide it is probably a measure of trust.

A focus on process improvement tends to reduce the significance of hierarchy, grade, status, differential technical knowledge and educational level. Even in the first stages of performance improvement initiatives like TQM, improvement suggestions based on tacit knowledge seemed to be offered on the basis of personal pride in the job, together with enthusiasm and pleasure at a new source of recognition of local expertise. This practice often did not last, though, as the organizational or behavioural context did not encourage it.

We asked the following questions:

• What makes an employee willing to offer tacit knowledge?
• Under what circumstances will this tacit knowledge continue to be provided on a regular basis?

The focus on process in performance initiatives such as quality management can generate a change in the relationship between work and learning. A considerable debate has developed as to whether or not TQM contributes fundamental organizational learning. In addition to the original quality gurus – Deming, Juran and Crosby – protagonists are customarily those who focus on the development of employee involvement in process improvement.[4] Antagonists are those who believe either that TQM does not go far enough to change the structure of power and remuneration in the firm, and therefore cannot make a major impact,[5] or that it is 'nothing more than a label for practices organizations are going through anyway'.[6] Our research indicates that performance improvement initiatives can at least create a potentially changed environment – giving employees a new perspective on work and learning. Collaboration can generate changes in work relationships, appearing to level grade, technical ability and education in the resolution of common problems, but it cannot be sustained unless the context supports these changes.

TQM does not in itself constitute fundamental organizational learning. At best it creates an opportunity, which can be attractive to employees. TQM and other performance-improvement initiatives may fail to take root for several reasons. First, they are often not effectively implemented because of inconsistent leadership and a lack of clear priority among numerous conflicting initiatives. Second, these initiatives often fail to encompass sufficient changes in the norms of behaviour to develop significant differences in the way things are done.

We further asked:

- What evidence is there that organizational learning may provide an opportunity for fundamental change in the organization?
- How is it possible to develop and sustain generative learning in an organization, or learning which will become permanent?

The need for the reform of human resource policies, to complement and strengthen performance improvement, has been recognized for some time.[7] Our research on employee involvement indicates that the human resource function plays an ancillary, sometimes supportive, always contextual, role in the change process.[8] Most of the major changes in our collaborating firms were driven by line management. Many firms initiated employee-involvement programmes which generated initial enthusiasm, reflecting an enhanced sense of involvement in perceived new responsibilities. Few employee involvement programmes have generated commitment to new organizational goals.

Commitment to corporate, division or even site organization was much less important than identification with and allegiance to the local work team in all our collaborating firms. Local commitment is of great assistance to performance improvement, which is essentially localized. But, as became obvious from both qualitative and quantitative findings, local allegiance is not sufficient if wider organizational supports are not in place.

While there was a significant reservoir of job involvement or individual identification with high levels of performance, the organizational environment and the perceived behaviour of managers prevented this involvement and identification from becoming more generalized or effective. Although a high proportion of our sample worked in teams, they tended to judge performance commitment on an individual rather than a team basis.

ICL MANUFACTURING/DESIGN TO DISTRIBUTION – SUCCESSFUL LEARNING

Listening to the people who worked in ICL/D2D gave an indication of how quality could become embedded in an organization and lead to fundamental change. Support for quality measures were so well developed that despite temporary diversions and setbacks generated by commercial imperatives, the significance of quality was never fundamentally questioned. From about 1990, it could always be refocused again with little loss of effort. Early on in the process, a supervisor recalled the quality circles in the mid-1980s,

> Many went along because it was a free hour, a tea break. I thought it was a waste of time. But now I've come to realize that without that long and continuous involvement, we could never have achieved what we are doing now in driving quality performance through the cells. Looking back it wasn't a waste of time. We concentrate now on corrective action teams and find them more effective and focused. It takes a long time to get people to believe in quality, but now it's accepted without question.

Alastair Kelly, managing director of D2D, always encouraged quality circles, initially without too much concern for their measured output or direct savings contribution. He thus realized the value of the process of learning, so aptly described by the supervisor.

Leadership, communication and management commitment

People in D2D worked with quality measures, structures, and reviews for ten years. Management avoided campaigns, preferring to drive quality through line managers. By 1987 every manager was expected to understand his or her role in the encouragement and development of quality improvement. Management commitment was demonstrated by teamwork, planned introduction of corrective actions, and opportunities to write and talk about the quality improvement process: 'We are seeking the permanent development of a culture and an environment where quality is a way of life,' wrote the division director as early as 1987. It was crucial that management understood their role. The leadership culture in the manufacturing division was described by a division manager as 'a strong value set based on task oriented results and risk taking, unfettered by rules and regulations which conflict with business imperatives'.

For the site general manager, Joe Smith, communication was vital: 'Tell them what you want from them and be clear about it. Ask them to contribute specifically to the process. They have a great deal to offer.'

Quality commitment was measured as a regular part of management assessment, as was the level of involvement of subordinates in quality teams. People were given a continuous stream of information on the business situation in which they worked (both corporate and site), and the difficult times the firm confronted in the global market. This communication was felt to be vital for helping to encourage a common set of goals.

Flexibility, responsibility and motivation

Alan Davies, the assembly manager, was regarded by management and operators as one of the best exponents of the new culture of openness and continuous flexibility. Davies was particularly well regarded by assembly operators for his ability to communicate and leadership qualities, and his sensitivity to individual abilities. In the assembly area, Davies introduced flexibility, in which operators moved from one work area to another, on the basis of their own assessment. 'We find the work so much more challenging,' said a team member. A group interview yielded some of the following further observations:

> From our routine line jobs, we have had to learn a lot of new skills. Alan was in the business of stretching us all. This gave us enormous confidence. If we couldn't do certain things we were discreetly moved to other tasks, no reprimand, no feeling bad about it.
>
> I like the work so much more now. It is a real challenge. Sometimes it's more stressful because you have more responsibility. I found that I was beginning to take the job home with me for the first time, worrying about decisions I had taken and recommendations I had made. But I wouldn't have it any other way. It is much more demanding; we find we get really committed to our work, and will work long hours if necessary.

From its introduction in 1985, the quality culture in D2D built consistency with new initiatives, strengthening those which had gone before. Although there may have been several times in the late 1980s when the drive for immediate financial results put quality temporarily in the background, its competitive significance to the firm has never been questioned.

THE SERVICE COMPANY – MIXED DRIVES AND TARGETS

By contrast, The Service Company had a typical programmatic intervention for quality management. It planned to involve people in quality through a corporate-wide involvement programme, the initial objectives of which were to introduce all employees to the basic elements of quality and problem-solving tools. The aim of the programme was to get people to solve their own problems and to introduce new responsibilities for work content, process and context. The programme was implicitly asking for a contribution of employee tacit knowledge.

Initial enthusiasm

In its early days, The Service Company programme was widely supported. People were talking of its potential for changing the culture and 'empowering' people, giving them a chance at last to contribute to their full capacity. Non-supporters of the programme felt it to be something which got in the way of regular business targets: supervisors in the firm reacted enthusiastically about their responsibility to introduce it to the line:

> Handled right, this could be the best thing to hit the company in the last 10–12 years. The programme should release energy and creativity in making the business more effective in meeting customer needs.
>
> If the commitment is not there from senior management, the programme will fail, and it will be seen by staff as just another 'flash in the pan'.

The senior ranks, however, left these front-line managers out on a limb: there was little recognition and support for the programme. At the same time as the programme was seeking to energize and involve people, quality targets were being driven in a parallel but unrelated process through the line. Because of a corporate-wide programme of delayering in 1991, job responsibilities had expanded at all levels of management. The achievement of short-term quality targets took precedence over everything. Front-line managers were trying to enlist the support of their managers for the involvement programme, while the company demands were pulling them in the direction of target results. The involvement programme was regarded as something which took time away from driving those results. While a questionnaire survey of front-line managers at the start of the programme revealed that quality and customer focus were felt to be deeply rooted in the culture of The Service Company, support for the programme, and its attempts to change the culture of the organization, began to wane.

Problems of organizational support

The involvement programme did not seem to retain the support it had when it was launched, although certain divisions kept a spirited effort in place, somewhat against the trend of the rest of the organization. The overwhelming drive for target performance, unrelated to the involvement programme, made it a low priority in most divisions. Our evidence from interviews indicated that the involvement programme was perceived to be largely 'counter-cultural' in the desire for measured performance improvement.

Not surprisingly, the programme began to atrophy after the first year because division management did not want to 'make it their own' by customizing or championing it, according to managers responsible for TQM. For most of the divisions, the involvement programme was considered simply a corporate programme which had to be 'signed off' in the quality reviews (ticking boxes of the number of meetings held and the number of people attending). There was little alignment of initiatives.

Major organizational changes in The Service Company the following year, including restructuring and reorganization, further split many working teams, disrupted the implementation of activities in the divisions, and dealt an additional blow to the programme. In addition to a lack of strategic focus and an excessive number of initiatives, the problems of lack of support from above, or the reward or recognition structure in the programme, were recognized by front-line and middle managers. Some managers felt that the programme had been a waste of time and money; many believed that continuous improvement should be management directed. Management in The Service Company seemed to be overwhelmed by the number of initiatives introduced by the company at any one time. The programme to get everyone involved in TQM was just another one of these.

AERCO PLC – POOR LEARNING OPPORTUNITY

Aerco PLC had quality assurance based on control and inspection (typical of the strict requirements for defence contracts) from the early 1970s. In 1991, in keeping with the trend in many UK companies, the firm introduced quality awareness training for the entire company. This was a comprehensive corporate-wide programme, and the first time anything so radical was attempted. Following the completion of training quality improvement meetings were set up throughout the plant.

Many teams identified barriers – principally, problems with others – to quality in the early weeks, but steadfastly refused to acknowledge any of their own defects. The use of language on the programme revealed evidence of a fairly well-entrenched blame culture. Since there was very little quality measurement in place, apart from the traditional fault reporting system, quality teams had no 'ownership' of targeted results. Group problem-solving skills were poor; most people had no experience of working in teams.

Problems of organizational support and communication

In several of the divisions there was poor support for involvement in quality improvement from top management, and poor awareness of leadership on the front line. As one director commented, 'How do you generate leadership from control management if it is not recognized as a problem?'

There was no quality review system for improvement activities in the first year, so few activities and little progress were recorded. The quality improvement activities had to operate within a rigid organizational structure based on a large bureaucracy built up in response to the initial defence work, and then perpetuated as the natural way to do things. To people on the front line, the organization seemed opaque, perhaps because of poor communication.

A number of major management changes, and restructuring, took place which were poorly communicated. Senior management made precipitous announcements about changing the function of charge hands on the line or bonus payments. The last issue was so poorly handled that supervisors sided with their people against management for the first time. During the research, there was a strike over some of these issues. Redundancies had destroyed the notion of job security in Aerco PLC.

Low trust

Trust between management and employees was very low. Together with the rigidities of the organization and an unchanged culture, quality improvement activities began to suffer. Poor teamwork skills, or local knowledge of the tools and techniques for process improvement, raised serious issues:

> Some people thought it was a waste of time. We were lacking in experience to take on a cross-functional meeting. There was poor communication between project managers and engineers. The task took a long time and people got discouraged.

On the shopfloor, people did not see the point of the quality activities. Many of them resented being taken from the line for the meetings. They also regarded it as a waste of time. Quality improvement activities failed to take root. The initial problem may have been a poor choice of programme, given the culture of the firm. But the most important and longer-lasting reason for failure was lack of trust and opaque organizational procedures. There was little clear understanding of what was required, and poor organizational support for assessing or recognizing local efforts. Little specific or organizational learning took place.

THE IMPORTANCE OF TACIT KNOWLEDGE

Tacit knowledge, or 'how' things are accomplished, is based on learning by experience. Conventional learning is based on training and skill acquisition, whereas tacit knowledge is knowledge embedded in a process. It customarily remains tacit – implicit in the way individuals do things. Employee tacit knowledge has become important to process improvement because technological change frequently makes jobs more, not less, complex. Thus it is increasingly difficult to monitor specialist work. In addition, the cost of replacing people, specially trained for a process in multi-tasking, is high. Employee responsibility takes on greater significance since there is less supervision because of downsizing and delayering. Continuous improvement, in any case, is based on localized activity.

Tacit knowledge has customarily been associated with technical innovation and technological transfer.[9] Originally it was based on the development of scientific knowledge and discovery. Tacit knowledge was

Table 4.2 Comparisons between tacit and specific knowledge

Tacit knowledge	Specific knowledge
Non-transferable	Transferable
Non-articulated	Articulated
Embedded (customarily)	Non-embedded
Episodic, procedural	Semantic
	Declarative
	Cognitive
Implicit	Explicit
Uncodified	Replicable
Embodied	Transferable
'Rules of thumb'	Routinized

deemed to be based on subjective personal experience, which is difficult to communicate. Tacit knowledge has been contrasted typically with specific knowledge, which is independent of the knower (see Table 4.2).[10]

Research revealed that while employee participation in performance improvement may be easy to develop on the basis of initial employee enthusiasm; it is also easy to destroy largely because of inconsistent policies, programmes or management behaviour. The institutional environment can determine the transaction cost of tacit knowledge, its tradeable value.

Offering tacit knowledge becomes possible because the traditional form of job control has little value any longer. As a tradeable asset (analogous to tacit knowledge in financial negotiations), it may be traded for relative or prospective job enhancement (skill/job flexibility).

EMPLOYEE TACIT KNOWLEDGE

Three examples of the provision of tacit knowledge, which developed into generative learning by changing the traditional norms of interaction in the workplace, are presented below. Each example illustrates a slightly different set of reasons for the provision of tacit knowledge. The last example is one of poor organizational alignment: the context for the provision of employee tacit knowledge became distorted by misunderstanding with management, and persistent low trust between employees and managers.

Example One: Fault information on printed circuit boards at ICL/D2D

In the manufacture of printed circuit boards for PCs, based on a complicated set of chemical and electronic processes with a highly varied technology/materials mix, employee teams at ICL Manufacturing had for a long time been dependent on engineering reports on the faults. In one of the first process improvement meetings in which they participated, employees asked to receive the direct printout of fault information, unanalysed by engineers, who had presented it in a form they did not understand. Using this basic data, employees were able to detect fault patterns which had not been previously recognized. Having the information, and the recognition of their potential expertise for solving particular faults on the line, they provided detailed knowledge on each stage in the process, to rectify faults on a continuous basis and raise further issues about the structure of the process and the optimal technology mix.

The provision of tacit knowledge is dependent on the ownership of information locally.

Example Two: Fissures in aircraft wings at Shorts Aviation

Shortly before he was to retire, an employee came to ask his supervisor if he should join the quality improvement training programme, since he would soon be leaving the firm after more than forty years. 'Oh, why not?' came the reply. He sat and listened to the first meeting which featured the contribution that employees could make to identifying and rectifying problems. He gave the matter some thought and in the afternoon began to talk about his job – one that he had done for more than ten years – of water testing and repairing the skins on the wings of Fokker aircraft (at the time, one of Short's major customers).

He said he thought that he had worked out a pattern over the last ten years of where these fissures appeared in the wing structure. He went on to describe it. He said that no one had ever asked him for his view on the matter. There had been two detailed investigations in this period based on aerodynamic assessment using computer models, but when the production engineers came to talk to the employee about rectifying the errors, he could not understand what they were talking about. They were not asking the questions in a way he could understand. So they left and nothing was done.

Shorts were able to save £250 000 per year on the basis of information provided by this employee, information collected iteratively which later become a replicable model. He left the company with a special citation from the chairman.

Releasing tacit knowledge is dependent on the context and the potential for mutual understanding in the identification of problems. It often fails to emerge because of technical or professional barriers which prevent communication between employees, who have specific expertise on the local context, and engineers who have the tools of analysis to rectify general problems.

Example Three: The operator certification scheme at Aerco

Savings on inspection were introduced into the manufacture of aircraft wing structures for the Airbus at an Aerco plant. Following a detailed training scheme, operators were given the responsibility of inspecting their finished work before it was handed on to the next process.

The inspection documentation was formal and prescribed, but the quality department soon discovered that a great deal of additional information was coming in to them on the back of the inspection forms providing detailed suggestions about how and why faults were occurring. At first they had no mechanism for dealing with this wealth of spontaneous information, but a line manager decided to develop a discussion meeting on it. Having been recognized as the people most appropriate to inspect the process, operators on the Airbus line began to feel responsible for a larger part of the process, and became willing to provide more than they were required on the basis of this recognition.

Making people responsible for quality, and trusting them in this process, provides an opportunity for the release of tacit knowledge.

Example Four: The anti-rollbar cell at Autopart Ltd

A prototype cell was established in this automotive parts manufacturer prior to the full introduction of cells on the line. Operators who participated in the experiment were enthusiastic about providing their suggestions on the design of the cell, particularly the positioning of machinery to optimize the process in the manufacture of a suspension part.

The operators had been led to believe that they would manage things themselves once the cell was established, which was contrary to the understanding of senior management in manufacturing. Thus when savings were made on the basis of process improvements suggested largely by operators working in collaboration with two young engineers, the prototype cell was criticized for being overmanned, and redundancies were made. The provision of suggestions based on tacit or other knowledge stopped, and eventually the pilot cell was disbanded.

In this instance both the enthusiasm and goodwill of employees for providing tacit knowledge was lost because of job loss, a poor delineation of boundaries of authority or recognition of a new structure based on participation.

TACIT KNOWLEDGE: AN OVERVIEW

Critical factors which encourage the provision of employee tacit knowledge are:

- information in a form which is useful
- well-structured opportunities for providing information
- clear instructions about what is needed
- collaboration and communication.

It seemed surprising that in some of the firms collaborating with the research, union shop stewards were among the first to promote employee-involvement schemes. This could be interpreted as the need to retain political control, but interview data revealed something different – a prime concern for the retention of members' jobs. The opportunity was there to revalue and gain respect for the work of employees, through consultation and the opportunity to contribute local knowledge.

Other research on tacit knowledge at work defined it as practical, rather than scientific, conscious or automatic, based on complex specificity, and determined by its context.[11] Based on a series of packers in a plant, it was found that they were able to achieve error-free calculations and least effort solutions. In work on computerized process control installations, success was achieved in those instances where the system was used to coordinate rather than control thinking.[12]

For what reasons do people want to provide tacit knowledge? We found that these reasons fell into two categories – what we called cognitive and credible explanations:

- *Understanding* was based on the individual role in process improvement and how it relates to the goals of the firm.
- *Credibility* was based on an assumption of the validity of corporate goals – an assumption which may involve trust in senior management.

Releasing employee tacit knowledge into process improvement on a regular basis requires fundamental changes in the way things are regularly done, including a fundamental shift of priorities – which are associated with organizational learning. More fundamental changes give rise to the opportunity for the development of alignment in the organization, based on the relationship of roles and responsibilities with the strategic priorities of the firm.[13]

In Figure 4.1 we combine learning, alignment and tacit knowledge. Competition in the 1990s can drive two types of reaction:

- *Programmatic intervention* through which tacit knowledge becomes apparent; but because the learning is reactive or adaptive, it may not be continuously provided. (The Service Company, Aerco PLC).
- *Strategic alignment* through which management models and operational practices are changed, generating a form of organizational alignment which becomes proactive or generative, making tacit knowledge available on a regular basis (ICL Manufacuring/D2D).

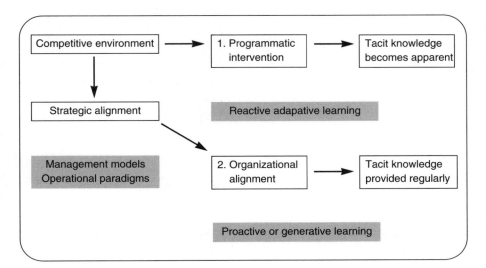

Figure 4.1 Learning, alignment and tacit knowledge.

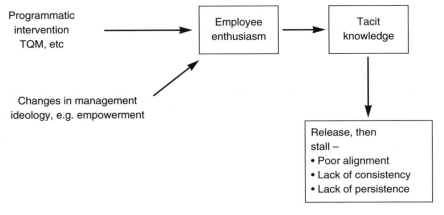

Figure 4.2 Releasing tacit knowledge.

Releasing tacit knowledge may be generated by employee enthusiasm reacting to a new performance initiative and a recognition of changed management ideology. Tacit knowledge does not become perpetual because of poor alignment, lack of consistency and persistence. Embedding tacit knowledge is achieved by developing both task and intrinsic alignment.

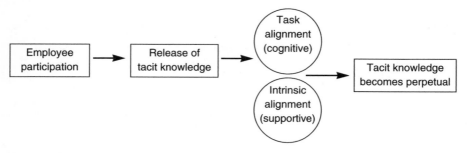

Figure 4.3 Embedding tacit knowledge.

FROM PROGRAMMATIC INTERVENTION TO EMBEDDING PERFORMANCE IMPROVEMENT

We have developed a three-stage matrix through which organizations might pass, from programmatic intervention to embedding performance improvement, including a set of identifiable changes in individual and organizational terms. These can be illustrated as in Table 4.3.

Stage One: Participation/programmed intervention

There is often considerable enthusiasm in the first stages of participation in programmes, even in fairly low trust firms. The participation process itself can become an affirmation of respect for local expertise, an affirmation of respect for work and knowledge. Tacit knowledge often becomes apparent for the first time at this stage, as people become willing to forgo the traditional job control of information, know-how and tacit knowledge on the basis of perceived changes in the organizational environment. This stage is characterized by programmed activities to generate a tentative form of motivation for improvement.

Table 4.3 Three-stage matrix

Stage One	Stage Two	Stage Three
Programmed intervention	Organizational learning	Embedded change
Release of tacit knowledge	Further release of tacit knowledge	Tacit knowledge becomes perpetual
Poor alignment	Task alignment	Intrinsic alignment
Participation	Involvement	Commitment

The Service Company demonstrated a good example of programmed intervention. Management had for years been attracted to one form of management fashion after another. Its front-line service people had become shrewd about judging these experiences, despite the size of the organization and the distance between them and senior management in terms of organizational grades and physical distance nation-wide. Corporate communication activities throughout The Service Company were continual and costly. They were prescribed in form throughout the organization and had become stylized in content and delivery. Most of the front-line people did not understand them.

People felt they had a clear concept of quality and customer service from the time when The Service Company had been a public utility. While they were initially quite pleased to go along with new service criteria and new plans to ensure quality, this, too, had been prescribed in form and structure by senior management. Some of the employees of The Service Company hoped that the corporate-wide quality improvement programme would at last provide an opportunity for them to give suggestions on how they perceived the customer service processes could be improved. Some indeed won prizes for their suggestions in a corporate suggestion scheme, but involvement in process improvement on the line rapidly lost support in the middle management ranks.

The Service Company failed to align employee involvement efforts to other targets for change and improvement which had been developed. Like other programmes before it, the involvement programme once launched was not sufficiently supported. This lack of alignment had been common in other previous activities of The Service Company, but this was the first time it involved such large numbers of people throughout the organization. What happened seemed to affirm people's view of the lack of consistency or credibility in senior managers.

Stage Two: Involvement/organizational alignment – a transitional phase

This stage relies on organizational learning on a more systematic basis than in the first stage, by integrating change initiatives and encouraging continuous feedback. It is the phase in which most companies get bogged down. Integration can promote an alignment of tasks through broad policy changes which become well accepted throughout the organization. Management consistency sets a stable agenda for change. More obvious and mutually acceptable boundaries between teams and functions are created, usually on the basis of newly defined processes. This stage assumes more self-generated improvement activities by each team, as greater understanding and more broadly based knowledge become apparent in the learning process. Tacit knowledge may become apparent through organized suggestion schemes or process improvement meetings. Continuous improvement may begin to be established.

The Defence Company had adopted a production system from the Kawasaki Group in Japan, used customarily for high-volume production of motorcycles or white goods, but in the case of The Defence Company applied to low-volume production of missiles. The Kawasaki Production System (KPS) required a complete restructuring of the plant based on just-in-time delivery and lean production. The KPS had made a considerable impact on changing the thinking of people in the plant, reaffirmed by new appointments to product centre management of those who favoured a more dynamic and participative style of leadership.

The Integrated Production Teams (IPTs), based on line teams together with engineering and design input, worked very well. For the first time, operators began to collaborate with engineers and could rectify process and other production faults immediately. Improvement teams based in the IPTs came up with hundreds of suggestions for taking cost out of the processes, improving tooling and enhancing the speed of production.

By creating a positive environment for cooperation across technical and function lines, The Defence Company had succeeded in changing the culture and operation of the plant very dramatically from a traditionally low trust inspection environment. Outside the structured activities of the IPTs, however, it was somewhat more difficult to get continuous improvement action groups established. Initially the operators were told that they would run them, but they were ill equipped to take charge of this complex process because of lack of training. Once taken over by engineers, however, the experience had become compromised. The initial energy and goodwill offered by employees was not matched by the training and experience required for performance improvement.

There was a discrepancy between the aims of culture change in The Defence Company and the reality of employee participation in these early days. While an excellent start had been made with the integrated production teams in KPS, this showed the potential which was not carried out elsewhere. The plant still had the feel of a 'them and us' culture. Management had developed a cognitive understanding of their improvement aims, but had not yet won their support. In too many instances operators remained temporary and marginal participants in the process. Thus while employee goodwill was obvious, with notable evidence of high job involvement, particularly among skilled workers, it had not yet been sufficiently tapped. The measures to take The Defence Company one stage further were based on alignment and training.

The Defence Company had made an excellent start by focusing change on a physical and structural layout of the plant through KPS which could be easily understood by people in this fairly traditional culture, but the lack of alignment prevented performance improvement from being embedded.

Stage Three: Commitment/embedded change

Characterized by positive factors of openness, communication, recognition and lack of blame culture found in the model of a 'high trust' company. Few companies observed have reached this stage, characterized by constant communication and a clear understanding of the balance between core policies and localized innovation. Alignment is perpetual and adjustment made on the basis of continuous change linked to common understanding. It is the stage at which tacit knowledge may become continuously available in the work environment, based on what might be called intrinsic motivation. It is this stage which offers the potential for generating innovation.

ICL Manufacturing/D2D introduced quality to the company about the same time as The Service Company. A crucial distinction was that quality performance was a key competitive factor in the computing industry world-wide. ICL could not afford to ignore it. The major impact of the quality programme over this period had been to align significant changes in the culture and operation of the company to quality. Management appointments and assessments were made on the basis of a contribution to quality. Teamwork collaboration on the line, while not always successful, had in the course of the decade become 'the way things are done around here'. Engineers were recruited particularly for their communication skills, and collaborated effectively with operators in cross-functional teams for process improvement, or in the delegation of regular maintenance and process improvement to operators.

Communication and frequent recognition were central to the changes that had been made at ICL. There was a lack of formality or distance in the interaction between operators and management, and a sense of common purpose based on out performing the world-wide competition had been achieved. Broadly speaking, ICL created a high trust company. Although certain problems always managed to challenge this situation, high individual motivation and a sense of common purpose were apparent throughout the firm.

The benefit of this type of performance change, and embedded performance improvement based on trust, was that ICL/D2D could count on a rapid and effective response to changes in the competitive environment. Responding to new customer requirements, for example, for a seven-day continuous working week when components arrived from the Far East until the product was out to market by assembly, was common. D2D had to become a thoroughly responsive organization to the demands of new and existing customers in the contract manufacturing business. Part of the success of their radical turnaround (from having been an internal supply division to ICL) is based on the success of embedded change and the capacity for continuous process innovation.

TRUST AND ALIGNMENT

The new economy gives new value to intangible assets such as the high motivation of people, which can develop in the course of corporate programmes. These are increasingly important to gaining competitive advantage. Recent books on strategy, corporate renewal and strategic purpose stress the importance of organizational and behavioural factors to maintaining the momentum of change. There has been a marked change in the management approach which acknowledges the contribution that people can make. We have tried to illustrate the prospects and difficulties of involving the workforce in improving performance on a continuous basis.

Our quantitative findings indicate that there is considerably more potential knowledge and goodwill than has been tapped by certain inconsistent attempts to generate corporate performance improvement.

Organizational learning is useful for identifying the type of effort which can begin to generate long-lasting change in an organization. Taking it one step further, organizational alignment helps an employee to relate his or her own effort to that of the firm – marking the potential for a new and more effective level of understanding.

Inconsistency of strategic and organizational initiatives can seriously weaken the potential for employee involvement. Thus there may be an enthusiastic response to the charismatic general manager who seeks to identify with the people by declaring 'We shall all be outside the factory gates, if we do not compete more effectively'. But the response does not last long if there is no further evidence to change the way things are done.

Tacit knowledge is one of the most valued contributions an employee can make to process improvement. The focus on process gives new prominence to work and learning, with the potential to promote new forms of cooperation. To provide tacit knowledge for process improvement may be seen as an act based on trust, as it is a negation of traditional job control.

Identifying with the strategic or other goals of the organization may also be based on trust – a new form of mutuality between employees and managers grounded in management competence and consistency, hence their credibility. Key variables which may develop and sustain the potential for embedding performance improvement are based on management integrity, communication/openness, fairness and recognition. All these form the basis of trust.

Table 4.4 The components of trust and alignment

Trust	Alignment
Integrity	Integration
Consistency	Consistency
Fairness	
Openness	Understanding goals
Competence	
Credibility	Constant communication

Let us look at the components of trust and alignment, which may help to illustrate their common qualities (Table 4.4).

Charles Handy wrote that trust needs boundaries (and clear understanding of its limits) and that trust demands learning.[14] Trust has an emotional as well as a cognitive side. The case study chapters which follow look at a variety of opportunities to build trust and effective performance improvement – illustrating how trust may develop step by step, but also considering work environments in which it will never prosper and others which have destroyed it.

REFERENCES

1 Senge, P. (1992) 'Building Learning Organizations'. *Journal of Quality and Participation* March; Kim, D.H. (1993) 'The Link Between Individual and Organizational Learning'. *Sloan Management Review* Fall; Moorecroft, J. (1992) 'Executive Knowledge Models and Learning'. *Journal of Operational Research* 59.

2 Argyris, C. (1992) 'Overcoming Organizational Defenses'. *Journal of Quality and Participation* March.

3 Argyris, C. and D. Shon (1978) *Organizational Learning: A Theory of Action Perspective*. New York: Addison-Wesley, 18–24.

4 Dale, B. and C. Cooper (1992) *Total Quality Management and Human Resources: An Executive Guide*. Oxford: Blackwell; Stephens-Jahng, T., B. Victor and A. Boynton (1994) 'Designs for Total Quality and Learning'. Technology and Management Innovation Division, Kenan-Flagler Business School, University of North Carolina, unpublished paper.

5 Lawler, E. (1992) *The Ultimate Advantage: Creating The High Involvement Organization*. San Francisco, CA: Jossey-Bass; Wilkinson, A. and Wilmott, H. (1995) *Making Quality Critical*. London: Routledge.

6 Pfeffer, J. (1994) *Competitive Advantage through People*. Boston MA: Harvard Business School Press.

7 Walton, R.E. and G.I. Sussman (1987) 'People Policies for the New Machines'. *Harvard Business Review* March–April; Wilkinson, A. and H. Wilmott, *op. cit.*; Hill, S. and A. Wilkinson (1995) 'In Search of TQM'. *Employee Relations* 17: No. 3.

8 Cruise O'Brien, R. (1995) 'Employee Involvement in Performance Improvement: A Consideration of Tacit Knowledge, Commitment and Trust'. *Employee Relations* 17: No. 3, 117.

9 Bell, M. and K. Pavitt (1993) 'Technological Accumulation and Industrial Growth: Contrasts between Developed and Developing Countries'. *Industrial and Corporate Change* 2: No. 2.

10 Polanyi, M. (1992) *Personal Knowledge: Towards a Post Critical Philosophy*. London: Routledge; Polyani, M. (1967) *The Tacit Dimension*. New York: Anchor.

11 Spender, J.C. (1993) 'Competitive Advantage from Tacit Knowledge? Unpacking the Concept and Strategic Implications'. Graduate School of Management, Rutgers University, *Academy of Management*, 9.

12 *Ibid.*, 11.

13 Beer, M. and R. Eisenstadt and B. Spector (1990) *The Critical Path to Corporate Renewal*. Boston MA: Harvard Business School Press.

14 Handy, C. (1995) 'Trust and the Virtual Organization'. *Harvard Business Review* May–June, 6.

Part II

The case studies in this part of the book offer the reader a snapshot of history from 1993 to 1995 when the strategic significance of quality was promoted in Europe and the United States. With hindsight we know that only one third of the companies which undertook quality programmes actually succeeded to any measurable degree and that the effort contributed very little to either productivity or profitability. The quality programmes tended to confuse means and ends or were bolted onto an unchanged structure. In some of the cases, it was clear that even though the production systems were radically altered the commitment of employees was not forthcoming because the cultures in these organizations had not changed. There was one positive example in our case studies – ICL/D2D – but the remainder of the firms with which I worked demonstrated a lack of consistency, openness or the alignment of front-line staff to the goals of quality performance. All displayed low trust, at varying levels.

The case studies offer lessons which lie at the heart of why companies fail to embrace new ways of working based on pushing responsibility downwards in the organization. They also consider why only a few firms became genuinely successful even in a campaign like total quality management, which was embraced by so many. Extensive interviews and observations of working teams underlined the prospects and difficulties of developing trust while working on performance improvement.

Leadership and commitment to change were critical factors in encouraging trust at ICL/D2D. A strong leadership culture was developed by people being promoted through the line with direct familiarity of the work processes. Information was communicated efficiently, with constant news about how the company was doing in the market. People were very familiar with the challenge they faced and could align this to the work that they were doing and the essential changes necessary. All these things contributed to an environment of trust. There was a culture of openness and frequent open meetings on performance improvement and the development of a culture of quality. People were given responsibility and flexibility in the work which they did. Local process information was available in a form which could readily be understood. Responsibility through the line was developed by task flexibility and the opportunity to change jobs. Surveillance was at a minimum. Despite the tough competitive climate, morale was good. Their Investors in People award reflected the efforts to develop the capabilities of people on the front line.

By far the most frequent cause of low trust in the other companies was the lack of information or poor communication from senior management. The Service Company had several programmes running at a time. People became cynical about the initiatives and did not believe the corporate information delivered on a regular basis. In some companies a 'rumour mill' replaced effective official communication. People became cynical about the absence of management commitment and consistency. In Autopart, they found management remote and uncaring. In both The Service Company and The Engineering Company they found senior management were taken with enthusiasms which they did not carry through.

Too often the changes which were being introduced cut across the corporate culture without making reference to the good things which had gone before. There was little enough effort 'to honour the past'. Some of the experiments or pilot schemes developed were set apart from the rest of the organization. These gave rise to jealousies and antagonisms, which often meant that they were disbanded. Several of the companies were described as having a firefighting culture where goals were unclear. And in several a 'them and us' culture prevailed. Blame was obvious in a few of the companies which practised little recognition for positive efforts made.

Enlarging the Scope for Change: ICL/D2D – Creating a High trust Firm

5

'In ICL you don't get in trouble for doing something wrong. You get in trouble for not doing something' (the personnel manager at the Ashton site of ICL Manufacturing).

ICL Manufacturing, which became Design to Distribution in 1995, was an organization that rose to the competitive challenge in the hardware industry in the 1990s principally by progressive policies of human resources and quality. Communication was a critical factor in its success. Total Quality Management was introduced in the mid-1980s and the company stuck with it. People on the front line were given responsibility and flexibility, and were supported in this effort. They were promoted through the ranks and the distinction between technical engineering staff and front-line people eroded in various team efforts which were product or process related. The unions went along with the programme. Trust was generated through all these activities which promoted the possibility of getting the best out of people. Commitment to quality was achieved in such an atmosphere with little effort.

RESTRUCTURING TO BE MORE RESPONSIVE

As a company ICL experienced a series of radical changes in the 1980s, necessary to turn it from a loss-making design and technology-driven company to a profitable one making equipment which was better designed for the customer and price competitive. Its strategic association with Fujitsu culminated in a take-over by the Japanese company (purchasing 80% stock from STC). This gave ICL vital financial security to restructure and create more ambitious strategic goals. ICL retained its separate identity in the partnership, while exploiting design, product integration and markets with Fujitsu.

Founded in 1959, International Computers Ltd was Britain's principal mainframe computer manufacturer. Throughout the 1970s redesign in the manufacturing process and late delivery were the norm. Once installed, a mainframe required almost full-time engineering assistance on-site. The Kidsgrove site (near Stoke-on-Trent) was opened in the early 1960s, and the assembly and test facility was based at Ashton-under-Lyme (near Manchester) in 1979. This plant established a very distinct 'Ashton culture' which in recent years has been recognized as an outstanding factory (UK Best Factory Award, 1989). Both sites participated in the research.

In 1980 the manufacturing division had a revenue of £100 million, no external customers, seven major factories and 7000 employees. In 1992, it earned £290 million, including £35 million from external customers in the two principal plants employing under 2000 people. In 1981, the pre-tax corporate loss of nearly £50 million required swift action to rectify low capitalization, a highly geared balance sheet, high fixed costs, and low earnings. The company needed to restructure, principally a shift from custom-building to standard packages, and from separate product areas (or engineering centres of excellence) to customer-based divisions.

The quality manager at Kidsgrove described the key to success in ICL at this time as 'having the skill to circumvent the system' and getting the product out. Building private networks through the dense bureaucracy that had become the management of manufacturing was the only way to get a product to the customer. In corporate terms, management had to be 'driven from its complacent negative approach, lacking in a profit motive, to a driving, "can do" culture obsessively focused on the bottom line.' The rapid changes in the computer market in the early 1990s focused their attention.

'The ICL Way' affirmed senior management commitment to the new vision in 1983, including management obligations based on several basic commitments:

- change
- customers
- excellence
- teamwork
- achievement
- people development

INTRODUCING EFFECTIVE QUALITY MANAGEMENT

Total Quality Management was introduced to ICL in 1986. The quality culture was built consistently and with new initiatives strengthening those which had gone before. Quality in ICL was driven from the top with consistent commitment from the then chairman, Peter Bonfield (now chief executive of British Telecom), and all divisional management. This basic commitment was never in question.

Most importantly, a 'critical mass' of support for quality had been established so that despite temporary diversions and setbacks generated by the commercial environment, quality was never fundamentally questioned. From about 1990, it could always be refocused again with little loss of effort. As a supervisor of the Process Production Centre, making computer boards, said of quality circles in the mid-1980s,

> Many went along because it was a free hour, a tea break. I thought it was a waste of time. But now I've come to realize that without that long and continuous involvement, we could never have achieved what we are doing now in driving quality performance through the cells. Looking back it wasn't a waste of time. We concentrate now on Corrective Action Teams and find them more effective and focused. It takes a long time to get people to believe in quality, but now it's accepted without question.

Alastair Kelly, managing director of the manufacturing division, always encouraged quality circles without too much concern for their measured output or direct savings contribution. By the mid-1990s more and more responsibilities were being pushed downwards because of delayering and downsizing, which was further confirmed by the move to self-managed cells. ICL began that task with a pervasive quality culture. Customer-based performance was built on consistently high-quality products delivered more quickly than those of the competitors. ICL designated Europe as its 'domestic market'. It was seeking to create a loyal customer base, through improved systems integration and more value added in sales and operations. From 1992 to 1994 the manufacturing division made a dramatic shift in its business from making exclusively ICL products to entering the contract electronics business. They introduced products for PC suppliers, particularly US multinationals. This placed exacting demands on all the manufacturing systems.

CHANGING COURSE IN MANUFACTURING

The division's first OEM (outside electronics manufacturer) customer was a major American workstation vendor in 1991, followed in 1992 and 1993 by three others, covering a range of equipment. In the manufacture of computer boards Kidsgrove's interconnect capability is seen as a unique selling point for new business, as well as multi-layer and multi-chip module technology giving the plant premier status in the UK and a major position in Europe. In state-of-the art integrated and completely automated lines for making printed circuit boards, ICL placed itself in direct competition for these boards with firms in lower-wage economies in the Far East. UK manufacture, of course, gave ICL's OEM customers a valuable location in the European market. But in the acutely competitive climate in computer hardware industry and the one-year design life of a PC, profit margins were exceedingly tight, and customer demands exceedingly exacting.

Gearing up to compete in the OEM business was a severe test of two principal factors of the manufacturing division: its capacity to deliver quality products in high volume for the first time, and its flexibility in having to deal with changing material and processes required by new contracts. The advantages to be gained from this new business for the manufacture of ICL products were improvements in the product introduction cycle from design to printed board, and the increased agility to meet fluctuations in demand through flexibility.

There were major redundancies in the division in indirect and direct staff, necessitated by the downturn of business and tight commercial situation during the 1990–92 recession. New commercial opportunities accelerated the need for a flatter, leaner management structure, particularly devolving more and more responsibilities to the shopfloor.

The Ashton site was assembling a new ICL PC made up of parts (components, boards, drives, boxes) from a manufacturer in Taiwan. They offered excellent delivered quality, a completely flexible workforce and better lead-time. Although Ashton (which had shrunk from 1000 employees in 1987 to 350 by 1995) was working with a core of minimal staff, they believed they could compete with firms in the Far East because of the flexibility and commitment of their workforce.

OVERCOMING THE BARRIERS ON THE FRONT LINE

Until 1993 Kidsgrove was exclusively an internal supplier to the manufacturing facility at Ashton. The turnaround to a high proportion of contract manufacturing business completely altered the structure, outlook and vocation of the Kidsgrove plant. The printed circuit assembly (PCA) area had some notable successes with contract manufacturing business since 1993, by introducing new automated and integrated lines which are increasingly characterized by a high proportion of operator process 'ownership'. But PCA supervisors had 70 direct reports with no approved structure of delegation beneath them. Spending an hour with a PCA supervisor involved almost continuous interruption from all over the floor. Relying informally on a few key people per shift, with no recognition or authority given to them, firefighting was continuous.

According to a manager in PCA, the problems of encouraging teamwork were that people became demotivated when meetings were cancelled because of a rush of work. 'They felt that we were not being serious about quality.' But most management in the area were convinced that the strident union heritage in this part of the factory was partly to blame for the lack of enthusiasm for teamwork. This was regarded as totally untrue by the quality line controller, who said that demotivation stemmed mainly from teams which worked for a number of months, and got no feedback from managers on the problems they raised.

Several teams were initially disbanded, but were reinstated under the leadership of new staff, who encouraged operator feedback, and became personally responsible for acting on suggestions. This continuous and reliable feedback on performance began to generate trust. In another example of demotivation from lack of follow through, statistical process control in the traditional line areas was introduced. Operators noticed that the SPC charts were not collected, so they stopped completing them. Their interest naturally fell away.

The quality line controller felt that the lack of feedback support or communication had devalued team efforts. He thought that people in PCA had high job involvement and really wanted to be consulted about how to run things, but there was no context for this to happen. 'If it is not encouraged consistently, an occasional meeting cannot generate it,' he said. This was certainly obvious from a 30-strong PCA quality meeting observed. In contrast to any other team observed on either site, and none as large as this, there was a lack of purpose, considerable embarrassment at raising issues, side-conversations and laughter, and an apparent blame culture, easily finding the opportunity to fault others for problems raised. The 'them and us' was still obvious, and almost no involvement had been achieved. This situation was obviously unsatisfactory, and well below ICL's own stated standards. In the course of 1993, contract manufacturing was radically transformed by an increased volume of business and a rapid expansion of jobs.

LEADERSHIP: INTEGRITY AND CONSISTENCY

The leadership culture in the manufacturing division was described by a division manager as 'a strong value-set based on task oriented results and risk taking, unfettered by rules and regulations which conflict with business imperatives'.

For the Ashton general manager, communication was vital: 'Tell them what you want from them and be clear about it. Ask them to contribute specifically to the process. They have a great deal to offer.' He had worked in IBM and Compaq before joining ICL in 1992 – a period of senior management recruitment at both sites, designed to help change the culture and outlook of the division. He set up the PCA area developing the first self-managed practices on-site. His principal supervisor, Alan Davies, had been a shop steward. Davies was promoted to the general manager's old job of production manager, and was regarded by management and operators as one of the best exponents of the new culture of openness and flexibility. Davies was particularly well regarded by assembly operators for his communication and leadership abilities, and sensitivity to individual aptitudes and capabilities. He proved supportive and strong and built confidence in unskilled assembly workers. He created an atmosphere of trust.

Management commitment was demonstrated by teamwork, planned introduction of corrective actions and opportunities to write and talk about the quality improvement process: 'We are seeking the permanent development of a culture and an environment where quality is a way of life,' wrote the division director as early as 1987 in *Quality Way*, the house magazine of the division.

Commitment to quality became a regular part of management assessment, measured as the rate of involvement of direct reports in quality teams. People in the division were given a continuous stream of information on the business situation in which they worked (both corporate and local), and were informed in detail of the difficult times the firm confronted in the global market. Communication was considered to be vital to allaying rumours and helping to encourage a common set of goals, according to management. Managers said that they felt as vulnerable as other staff.

INVESTING IN PEOPLE

ICL won the Department of Employment Investors in People award in 1993, based on progressive human resource policies:

- 'the right skills in the right place' to release the potential of the workforce
- a reward system based on recognition
- a new framework for delivering corporate goals
- an appraisal process assessing the degree of internalization of those goals.

The company's Investing in People programme was introduced in 1988, as part of a strategy to improve business performance through increased employee involvement. Harmonization of conditions across all grades, including holiday entitlement, sick leave, pension and private medical care, was an initial part of that programme. Surveillance was at a minimum – people no longer clocked in, nor were they monitored on breaks by supervisors. All these measures contributed to trust.

Management guides included the need to develop the individual capability of employees. These guides were used as a source of management training. Copies of documentation were well annotated, and supervisory staff mentioned how helpful these had been 'when they were thrown in at the deep end'.

An observer at the time wrote:

> I was greatly impressed by the commitment of line managers to developing people management skills and the conception of managing line workers by 'bringing them out', extending their skills and getting them to carry greater responsibilities. Line workers interviewed believed their supervisors to be responsible for pushing them towards responsibilities they never dreamed they could reach.

Operators worked a 37-hour week on a flexible basis, which was helpful to working women with children. A high proportion of the assembly employees on both sites were women. Their high proportion in the Ashton plant generated the following observation by the personnel manager on gender differences:

> Women have handled the ambiguities in the work environment better than men operators. They are less confrontational, less focused on personal gain and status. They think that flexibility is a totally sensible way to work, and show continuous willingness to help. Most of the problems they raise are relationship problems which affect the collective.

Throughout informal interviews with shopfloor staff in the assembly area at Ashton the 'employer brand' seemed to be quite strong. Although some local electronics firms paid better base rates, none could compete with the package which ICL provided. Progressive human resource policies impacted favourably on the possibility of developing trust.

INVESTING IN SKILLS AND QUALIFICATIONS

Following harmonization, new career structures were introduced for professional and technical staff. The most important changes were the recognized addition of new areas of management and inspection responsibilities on the shopfloor. For appraisal purposes, the aptitude for basic problem solving and teamwork skills were introduced. New job descriptions included added responsibilities for production output, breakdowns and maintenance. The new grades had a set of added responsibilities linked to each job. This expansion reflected both responsibilities for quality assessment and monitoring and a move towards self-managed work teams. New forms of employee involvement were written into contracts.

Some difficulties were expected from the unions because new responsibilities were added without a pay award, but it was generally believed that the people themselves were willing to accept. First, it made their jobs more varied and interesting; second, task flexibility, which implied new forms of training, enhanced the potential of job security. This was based on the assumption of wider areas of responsibility, giving pause for consideration when the next round of redundancies arose. The division training programmes evolved from one-off offerings to personal and career development. All these changes enhanced trust at a time when the demand for production quality was high.

RECOGNIZING PERFORMANCE ON THE FRONT LINE

To achieve its commercial aim, the Ashton plant moved towards what its general manager called a 'virtual factory', based on networked resources in manufacturing which were totally flexible, an unambiguous commitment to building individual and group potential, a shared vision and a willingness to experiment with new manufacturing methods. This was based on an understanding of business objectives by all employees on-site. The challenge was to encourage a flexible workforce, ensuring mobility between the shop-floor and services. The peaks and troughs of production could only be effectively serviced if everyone was willing to do all jobs on demand. Test engineers, for example, packed equipment if necessary.

The middle management team at Ashton was transformed by recruitment of new talent from the shopfloor. In contrast to the effects of promotions of this kind in a traditional factory context, the new management at Ashton did not join the 'white-collar' grades and create distance between themselves and their direct reports. Instead they maintained excellent communication with working teams, and used their detailed knowledge of people's abilities to move them with a flexible work environment, and thereby stretch their innovative and organizational abilities as well as their skills. According to extensive informal interviews with assembly staff at Ashton, building trust had a positive effect on the acceptance of change as well as commitment to quality performance.

EMPLOYEE SUGGESTIONS

A traditional ICL corporate suggestion scheme was introduced in the early days of quality training and awareness. It became obvious that there was an increasingly lower level of suggestions each year. Interest waned largely because the management response was exceedingly slow. The principal problems were: the slow procedures, lack of promotion of the scheme, lack of standard procedures or mechanisms for prompt implementation, and no panel for evaluation. Critical to the downturn of the scheme was the general lack of support from supervisors and managers, who gave it a low priority.

Following a visit of senior corporate management of ICL to a number of Japanese companies in the early 1990s, a Japanese-style suggestion scheme, called dELTA, was launched company-wide. The principal goal of senior management was to use this system to enhance motivation and involvement in quality. Cost savings generated by the scheme were considered to be of lesser importance.

Under the new scheme, employees were encouraged to make as many small suggestions as possible. The underlying objective was that everything could be improved, and that the company had a great deal to learn from everyone's ideas. The scheme supported the notion that the best ideas came from the people closest to the processes themselves, and that a blame-free culture based on trust was essential to its success. The manager role in the dELTA process was supposed to enable people to express ideas and empower them to implement their proposed solutions.

The main problem which the production centre management on the front line had with the new scheme was how to cope with the volume of suggestions put forward. The number of suggestions recommended by division management for each employee was 25 per year (modest by Japanese standards) giving supervisors with 60–70 direct reports, a substantial additional workload. The objectives of the scheme were continuous improvement, high level of participation and implementation and fast response.

The benefits were outlined as

- enabling fast organizational change
- creating a 'learning organization'
- improving motivation, communication and pride
- supporting customer care
- supporting quality improvement.

The problems with the scheme were again principally to do with management support and response. It raised the question whether or not Japanese corporate culture had a number of interrelated factors which supported such a scheme, making it less adaptable to British firms if plucked out as a single initiative. Management commitment once again proved difficult to obtain because of competing pressures. Newsletters were circulated throughout the year to bring people up to date on the scheme. Retaining the momentum of such a scheme became a constant challenge.

After the scheme had been running for a year, it attracted about thirty suggestions a week, although there remained a concentration of activity in certain areas. The simplified version for dELTA was also more accessible on the shop-floor, which assisted in raising participation. A manager who developed the schemes said 'No matter how well we designed the scheme, the bells and whistles lost their impact after a while'.

COMMUNICATION

The preferred method of internal communication, identified by the annual ICL Employee Survey, was the team meeting. Team meetings were weekly or *ad hoc* meetings covering principally quality performance and production targets. Each month a team brief was cascaded down from divisional management on the same day, and used to open team meetings. This form of communication came next in popularity as the preferred means of communication. Notice boards were also identified as an important source of information. ICL was very keen on many visible notice boards measuring quality progress, such as Corrective Action and Error Cause Removals currently in play, trend improvements in quality, notable achievements of particular teams or individuals and corporate quality information. Each department featured in a prominent place the name and photograph of the local coordinators. It had the forms for Corrective Actions and Error Cause Removals, and often had photos of the local quality improvement team. The dining hall featured a very large photo of all employees on Zero Defects Day with a signature (a pledge?) from each. Notice-board visibility had often been mentioned as important in quality companies like Rank Xerox and Nissan, UK. It was certainly evident in ICL.

MOTIVATING THE TEAM

A few quality circles had won special commendation: the Michelin award for 1991 was given to a quality circle which invented a tool, subsequently patented, for extracting bonding plates from boards (an important industry-wide contribution); in 1992 a vendor quality circle perfected a ship-to-stock scheme also earning commendation. Quality circles were generally regarded as an important part of history at ICL by both operators and management.

Essential as they were to raising the awareness of quality and encouraging people to participate in teamwork, awards were eventually considered much less important than corrective action (CATS). These were generated through a formal procedure, or driven by the price of non-conformance (PONC). They were mandatory, designated to solve a particular problem, and were cross-departmental or functional. From 1986 to 1990, a number of CATs suffered from lack of focus, structure and training, according to quality staff in both plants. A number of teams began with very large and complicated general problems which retarded initial progress. This tended to discourage participants. From 1991 a great deal of effort has been made to refocus CATs to key business issues by linking them more closely to performance measures. With hindsight, quality and line management agreed that it would have been preferable to have offered some guidance to the teams initially. This would have helped them to identify problems which could be solved relatively easily in the first instance to ensure a quick early success that would have further encouraged the corrective action process.

The next stage of team activity was for teams to form and disband much more informally. Moving towards self-managed work cells, this new flexible teamwork environment was intended to deal with the problem as close to the line as possible to encourage an efficient team environment for solving problems promptly and efficiently.

TRANSFORMING A WORKING TEAM

Flexible working

Given the reduction in product life cycles, materials receipt and storage had to become very flexible to deal with business demands. It was essential to maximize operator flexibility and provide substantial extra training so that each employee became familiar with all the areas. Job flexibility in stores began with a skills matrix assessment. Previously the workforce of twenty-six at the Ashton plant had been fixed into four areas. Their lack of flexibility, according to the stores manager, affected quality performance. A new appraisal system was based on extra tasks, each with a small proportion of what was previously supervisory work, such as space utilization, barcode implementation, and database design.

The new organization in stores reduced overtime, increased the length of service to the line as needed, and helped to introduce proactive day-to-day resolution of quality issues. Flexible work practices were introduced to match the 'pull' or demand from assembly. People did not react negatively to these changes, which now involved weekend work as well as longer hours. The additional training and flexibility made people feel more secure in their jobs. Under the old system there was little room for advancement. Through new job flexibility people began to come up with many new ideas. In such a low-tech work environment, operator knowledge of systems and routines was of high value. According to the stores supervisor, flexibility created new opportunities for motivation and teamwork.

Communication

While the most fundamental changes were being introduced the stores manager was in the department throughout the day in constant communication with people, thus able to field new ideas immediately and help with training. Each day's departmental meeting was a forum for customer issues, feedback and suggestions. The department was run on a daily basis by the supervisor. Teamwork with people in purchasing helped to build new relationships and create an arena for cross-fertilization of ideas. Each cell began with a 'kick-off brief', which was started when Ashton was preparing for the European Quality Award Assessment. Cross-functional teamwork between assembly and stores helped assembly operators to understand extra-departmental problems and to resolve problems between departments. As one stores operator commented, 'Now we know the stores people and we depend on them more. We interact with them and form a team. They come to ask us about the versatility and robustness of various parts we use. It is a responsibility.'

Results

People on the line were proud of their contribution to the quality process, and their responsibility to reject items that did not meet quality criteria. They were often indignant when production pressures led line managers to encourage them to relax quality standards. Each of the three cell leaders was responsible for the procedures, performance statistics and measures for each area. Although none had had this kind of experience before, they were also expected to take responsibility for process control and problem solving.

The quality circle process had a 'hidden agenda' – to try to identify new natural leaders and begin to promote their legitimacy among their peers. Those with a natural aptitude for leadership would not only be identified but recognized by others through the process, and not therefore seen as management appointments. Newly identified team leaders attended a two-day course in teamwork. Team leaders interacted directly with customers. They had quality and output targets.

By contrast, there were parts of the Kidsgrove site which demonstrated relative low trust between the supervisory and operator roles, or between engineers and operators. As one product centre manager at Kidsgrove said, 'We rationalized the organization (delayered, giving supervisors large process rather than function responsibilities) without looking at the aptitudes for the job'. There was still a heavy remnant of blame culture, a lack of common acceptance of core goals. In such an environment, the unions became active again because of dissatisfaction generated by uncertainty and change.

MAKING PEOPLE RESPONSIBLE

The Process Product Centre manufacturing computer boards was headed by a manager who joined the company during a new intake of senior managers. He had previously been with Digital where he had worked with empowered teams. In the line organization, he had enlarged the responsibilities of supervisors to include production targets and quality measures. He introduced cell management based on these key operator functions. A reassessment of supervisor capabilities, following the delayering in 1992, was essential to ensure delegation, and give the supervisory role additional responsibilities for quality, production and engineering.

To ensure that the campaign was successful, supervisors with aptitudes and skills which fitted the new structure were used. There was a need to refresh the tools and techniques used by operators, and 'create a proactive organization'. Achieving objectives such as scrap reduction was believed to require new elements of self-management. Key operators were appointed with salary increments. Success of scrap reduction was based on a move to cell self-management led by key operators. Getting responsibility as close as possible to the production unit was essential to success. The provision of information directly to key operators was an important element. KOs cited the significant difference this made to their understanding of process problems, especially scrap. That they no longer had to rely on engineers for the same information ('delivered in a way we didn't understand anyway') was significant recognition of their new responsibilities for output and quality. 'Giving operators direct access to information meant that the engineering mystification was removed. They were now more aware, and therefore more responsible. And they welcomed it.' According to a supervisor: 'One of the three components of self-management is information. The others are knowledge and authority. Information can be a powerful motivator.' Pushing responsibility to the front line was a good motivator and a source of trust.

One of the fundamental components of this climate for change was an understanding of where people fitted in the structure. Although there was considerable de-skilling on both sites, 'people needed to know where they fitted, what they contributed and what their targets were', according to the general manager at Ashton.

New forms of motivation developed in the Assembly area by the introduction of flexibility in which operators move from one work area to another, on the basis of their own assessment of demand. 'We find the work so much more challenging' said a team leader. This climate of high motivation was essential to all the demands for quality performance.

The key to trust building in ICL/D2D was a combination of factors, including progressive human resource policies, effective communication, flexibility and the award of responsibility to the front line. The consistency and openness of management was also critical to the success of sustaining trust. The road was not always a smooth one, but the drive and singleness of purpose borne from their competitive market made trust an essential asset.

Sacrificing Trust: Too Much Change Too Fast at the Service Company

6

RESISTING CHANGE

> People like working for this company, but they are disillusioned. They are loyal.
>
> Old strengths of our organization are being lost like the dedication of staff to their work and the informality of staff communication.
>
> We've been 'over-videoized' and over-patronized.

These are some comments made during quality training in The Service Company in the early 1990s. Throughout the 1990s the company instituted a plethora of changes which often left people disillusioned. They had a strong impact on traditional loyalty in the organization and impeded the building of trust. While organizations may respond to change quickly, they integrate change much more slowly. Ignoring the corporate culture can create a considerable undertow. People in The Service Company believed themselves to have high traditional job involvement, pride in work and a historic attachment to their public service culture, which they perceived to be based on excellent customer service and quality. Inevitably, dissatisfaction led to a lot of idealizing of what went before.

Whether or not it was valid, it became part of the corporate folklore: 'We have always had quality, and a high level of customer service. Management used to be closer to us, more visible, more responsive.' The strength of loyalty was based on the fact that most of the people spent their working lives in The Service Company, having received all their training in the company. People were incredibly loyal. 'Next to family, The Service Company has been the most important thing in my life,' commented an engineer.

Low trust in senior management was matched by little pride in working for 'the new Service Company'. The employees had limited identification with the corporate vision and did not believe most corporate communication. These attitudes led them to be resistant to change in an atmosphere of limited communication, leading to an overactive rumour mill. They initially rejected involvement in the quality programme. To be more credible, the cultural change programme might have retained some of the corporate values understood to be important to The Service Company employees, and on the basis of which they traditionally exhibited high levels of loyalty. A culture change programme which cuts across such strongly held beliefs usually fails. In trying to foster culture change, The Service Company in the 1990s failed to give due honour to the past organization. Changes in the way people think form the basis of change in an organization. It is most effectively based on a consistency between what people experience and what they understand. Inconsistency proved a serious barrier to change. It had a high impact on the potential for building trust.

> Where are the people values? Some people have insulated themselves rather than live in fear. It does not lead to involvement or trust.
> Are The Service Company values changing? We respect each other, but does the chairman respect us?

THE QUALITY IMPROVEMENT PROGRAMME

> The programme should release energy and creativity and make the business more effective in meeting customer needs.
> If the commitment is not there from senior management, the programme will fail, and it will be seen by staff as just another 'flash in the pan'. *Handled right*, this could be the best thing to hit The Service Company in the last 10–12 years.
> Most important is that the impetus for the programme is maintained by continuous backing from the top, without constantly introducing different and apparently contradictory policies.

Despite a poor context for trust and commitment, The Service Company's quality improvement programme was one of the most radical and ambitious employee involvement programmes in the UK in the 1990s. It was initiated and piloted in 1988 following management TQM workshops across the company. In 1990–91 a restructuring and delayering effort took precedence over all corporate programmes, in an effort to finally get away from the twelve layers of management under which it had previously operated. The quality programme was launched in 1991, to a resonance of 'At last!' and 'About time!'

The Service Company had a poor record of consistency for corporate programmes. People were neither surprised nor particularly concerned, therefore, that the programme was suspended for six months shortly after it had started.

> We seem to celebrate beginnings, not endings in The Service Company. We don't usually hear about the results. Dedication further up the ladder seems to be lacking. Our staff are aware of these stops and starts. They went to the quality–improvement programme with a cynical view.

Attention focused instead on the largest redundancy programme yet in Britain when 25 000 people left the company

Front-line managers had principal responsibility for the quality programme, 'empowered as its leaders' and given a detailed manual. The tools of empowerment were authority, information and support. But support from middle and senior management was always felt to be lacking. It was never altogether clear if the programme had priority despite the lip service paid to its importance. Front-line managers had difficulty with their new responsibilities, particularly because of poor morale in the organization at the time. They were battling against the odds to create a new outlook.

PUSHING TARGETS OR INVOLVING PEOPLE: A DILEMMA

At the same time as the programme was seeking to energize and involve people, quality targets were being driven in a parallel and unrelated effort through line management. Because of downsizing in 1991, job responsibilities had expanded at every level. Front-line managers were trying to enlist the support of their own managers, who felt overwhelmed by the demand for target results which had little to do with the programme. The situation left the front-line managers out on a limb.

> Unfortunately not everyone in the company is committed (I include both managers and non-managers). There will therefore be a reluctance to participate, and if we are not careful, it will fail. Quality should be part and parcel of our everyday work – a programme like this should not really be necessary.
>
> Feedback is something which is sadly lacking in The Service Company generally, a great shame because the concepts behind quality programmes are extremely exciting for me and the company.

In its early days, the people who supported the programme were talking of its potential for changing The Service Company culture, of 'empowering' people, of giving The Service Company people a chance at last to contribute to their full capacity. Non-supporters of the programme felt it to be something which got in the way of regular business targets. Some senior managers were very supportive, but it did little to provide systematic support through the line.

Forty centres for the quality programme were established throughout the country, which would receive the entire non-management workforce in a period of eighteen months. These events were the first time people met with colleagues from other divisions of the company. At the day event people were seated at tables of eight to ten, presided over by a front-line manager. Following an introduction to the mission and values of the company, exercises focused on the characteristics of a 'quality company'. Participants were introduced to group problem-solving techniques, watched corporate videos on quality and finally did a simulation exercise. There was a link between the one-day event and exercises on customers and suppliers back in each working team. The 'day out' was a success for a great majority of participants, some of whom were reluctantly brought into the fold though the persistent efforts and encouragement of front-line managers.

The teamwork exercise back at work was much more testing in terms of effective delivery. It was intended to generate continuous improvement. While in principle the programme was thoughtfully designed, it met several problems:

- Responsibility for the teamwork exercises foundered because of the pressure of work.
- Despite structural change and empowerment, the command control structure of the company remained largely unchanged.
- Managers struggled with leadership skills, having spent most of their working lives in a hierarchical bureaucratic structure. They had few personal resources to inspire their people.
- Poor morale and job insecurity naturally affected people's willingness to participate in the programme.

Successful culture change might not only honour the past, but also understand such problems and the perceptions on which they are based if it is to create a new basis of credibility and change. The problems which became obvious in The Service Company were: the integrity, consistency and competence of senior management, leading to poor morale. While micro-cooperation based on teams could be successful, people retained an exceedingly poor view of the corporate management. Official company statements contrasted sharply with morale (Figure 6.1).

PROBLEMS OF MOTIVATION AND MORALE

The Service Company must not only 'preach' and state values, they must work to them and show, by example, the quality – from the top.

- We put our customers first
- We are professional
- We respect each other
- We work as one team
- We are committed to continuous improvement

Figure 6.1 The Service Company's values.

This is still not apparent in everyday work. Too many 'poor-quality' decisions and events currently overshadow any quality attempts by groups.

The message from board level will fail, as it did before with the vision, mission and values because the managers involved are unable to translate the message into what it means to people at the lower levels.

The attitude from senior management towards lower grades is not all it should be. Lower grades are intelligent enough to realize that massive changes are imminent, but the facts are being withheld, and things which will have lasting effects on future prospects are being glossed over.

This is in the hands of top management. If we are in a state of continual change and uncertainty, then it will be difficult to gain confidence of the staff and get their full commitment.

A 1992 survey found some issues of fundamental importance for corporate programmes in The Service Company. Front-line managers generally felt that the quality improvement programme had great potential and clearly welcomed the responsibility for administering it. They felt that they would have to work hard to overcome the problems of morale and job insecurity, which seemed so acute at the time of roll-out. Like front-line employees, they were sceptical of senior management's commitment to the programme, demonstrated particularly strongly in responses to the open questions.

While only 16% of front-line managers felt that their people were enthusiastic about the programme, 95% felt that their team would be willing to put themselves out for a good job. This reflected very low support for corporate programmes and very high perceived job involvement. Job involvement (perceived or actual) was declining. The continuing job insecurity and uncertainty or confusion surrounding reorganization were the principal factors affecting this.

Special meetings between middle managers and front-line engineering employees were arranged so that managers could learn first-hand about specific customer and process problems. The first two meetings were very confrontational, and very little was accomplished. By the third monthly meeting the atmosphere began to change, and people were encouraged to identify key problems.

The experience turned at the fourth and fifth meetings when front-line staff began to identify with management, acknowledging, for example, difficulties in taking up suggestions for financial or technical reasons. Managers suspended the meeting after the fifth one, believing them to be of limited usefulness. The employees were angry and disappointed considering the effort they had made. The middle ground created quickly disappeared. The whole episode was a major setback in the relationship between engineering staff and managers.

INTERVENTION NOT SUPPORTED THROUGH THE LINE

The general morale in the organization, as well as the poor support from senior management, left front-line managers isolated in their efforts to involve people in quality. There was, of course, a significant minority of middle management who believed in the importance of the quality improvement programme for supporting continuous improvement. They were very supportive, but in the minority.

> I have practised a form of TQM for years. I am a strong believer in letting people have a say how they work. My only slight concern is The Service Company's way of tackling this is rather formal, bureaucratic and time consuming.

The two most important outcomes of the quality programme, according to front-line managers, were felt to be team awareness of quality and additional responsibility for the team. It could be said that the first was achieved only partially because awareness in most cases was not reinforced by team activity in the workplace, which could have contributed to continuous improvement. That the teams would have additional responsibility was probably a misunderstanding of the aims of the programme. The substance of the programme could have generated additional responsibility for the teams if the management and corporate culture had been more supportive. Trust was in short supply.

THE ALIGNMENT OF MANAGEMENT THINKING

The specific problems of the quality improvement programme were a lack of alignment between quality and other initiatives and the commitment and ownership of line management. Further, many managers felt they had been progressively 'disempowered' by other policies and practices, particularly financial controls, making it difficult for them to 'empower' people.

In the view of many people in The Service Company, the purpose of the quality improvement programme had been somewhat deflected from getting people actively involved in continuous performance improvement to an attempt to rebuild morale. Some observers indicated that it was not even possible to improve morale in certain teams, although other teams got beyond the morale issues to improvement projects. Before research was completed, I was told by a senior manager in one of the divisions that the quality improvement programme was 'dead'. This, he felt, was largely because of competing priorities which had begun to take precedence and continuous restructuring that had repeatedly disrupted the stability of work teams.

The number and range of change initiatives introduced in The Service Company in the last ten years has streamlined many practices and changed the culture of the organization. But the most important problem in The Service Company seemed to be a lack of consistent identification of priorities, alignment of management thinking accordingly, and clear messages going out through the organization about the core goals and direction of change. TQM is only one set of programmes in a long line of improvement activities.

People were made aware of quality, but not given responsibility for it. The programme began to atrophy by late 1993 because most of the divisional executives did not want to 'make it their own' by customizing or championing it, according to managers responsible for TQM activities. For most of the divisions, the programme was considered simply a corporate programme which had to be 'signed off' in the quality reviews. Management reviews of sessions often became an exercise of 'ticks in boxes' or being satisfied with quantitative verification that the sessions had taken place (based on observation). Some divisions had 'soft audits' and facilitation for a sample of these activities with working teams, which helped to maintain some of the momentum.

Organizational changes after this period, including restructuring and reorganization, further split many working teams, disrupted the implementation of activities in the divisions, and dealt an additional blow to the quality improvement programme. In one of the few divisions which was making an elaborate effort to re-kickstart the programme, 'making people proud again to work for The Service Company' was felt to be an important current issue for the general manager.

The programme generated greater awareness of quality throughout the organization, but the effort to create ownership of quality was scarcely achieved. There were numerous success stories but these were generally exceptions to the rule.

More often the losses were counted. First was the cost of the quality programme and the professional time invested in initiating and implementing it through eight team sessions. Additionally the losses were the management of change potential of front-line management, the capability of working teams whose members believed in the potential benefits of the programme and poor morale in the organization through disappointment. The sceptics were proved right; the organization did not really support the programme to its conclusion.

The Service Company continued to manage change in a largely directive mode. It had, however, altered management selection and recruitment in order to foster change, without perhaps providing the sustained tools and support to enable them to manage that change. This partial achievement of change had a strong impact on the prospect of developing and sustaining trust.

Poor Communication and Uncertain Boundaries Impact on Trust at Autopart

7

MANAGEMENT UNCERTAINTY AND COMPETITIVE DEMANDS

Good ideas and intentions for change at Autopart were sabotaged by poor support from management. People became involved and excited about the new self-managed work teams programme, but the management did not have a consistent view on support for the changes which were essential to its success. The boundaries of the experiment were not clear, as autonomy was not necessarily recognized by management. People were unsure what constituted success in the experimental teams, as accurate information was not forthcoming. The firefighting culture persisted alongside unproductive team meetings in some parts of the plant. The most significant downside of the experiment for the workforce was that an increase in productivity led to job loss and overtime pay reduction. People naturally felt betrayed as the outcome of their efforts led to this. Low trust and a poor assessment of management was the result. People recognized that management needed to maintain control.

In the Autopart factory you could see the whole production operation from the front door of the plant, yet it was one of the most low trust environments of the research. Founded before the Second World War, Autopart makes rubber-bonded components for car suspension systems. In the early 1990s the MD made numerous visits to Japan, and was impressed by the size of the production units, using smaller tools and presses which encouraged flexibility. Among Autopart's most important customers at the time were Volvo, Ford and Mercedes-Benz.

Autopart felt the power and demands of competitiveness in the industry.

Their product life was about five years, so 20% new business must be found every year to 'stand still'. At the time of research, Autopart was moving to cell manufacturing with the help of prominent engineering consultants and adopting a new business operating system, substantially based on the Ford Quality Operating System. Autopart had to be persistently reactive to its most powerful customers.

Nissan (UK) and Ford were among the most demanding on quality. On the basis of a single part fault for Ford, Autopart were required to demonstrate a detailed internal management assessment of their processes, leading to corrective action. Ford required all suppliers to introduce parallel quality assessment systems to their own, and typically used this as a vetting procedure for reducing the number of suppliers used.

NEW INITIATIVES BUT LACK OF CLARITY

Employees contributed good ideas to the continuous improvement process, but these were slow to receive attention. The culture was not conducive to providing ideas on a continuous basis. Only 20% of Autopart employees felt that their managers encouraged people to make suggestions compared with 70% in the global research sample. It was assumed that the new cell management structure would promote improvement suggestions. Cross-functional problem solving teams showed promise for capturing individual contributions to process improvement. Teamwork was minimized by limited proficiency in all but the basic problem-solving tools. The gradual maturing of both line and problem-solving teams made it possible to capture not only improvements but also potential innovation.

Group managers in the new cells had pivotal new roles. They were designated change agents, yet the parameters of their authority were not fully worked out. The director of manufacturing was concerned about the need to make the group managers commercially aware, and give them basic financial skills. The cells were intended to be 'stand-alone businesses'. But the lack of clarity was a serious drawback to the functionality of the new structure in its initial phase. A negative precedent was set in the team initiated as a pilot cell. The experience was largely a failure because the parameters of team authority were again not clearly defined. The definition of boundaries is crucial to successful cell manufacture and to the development of trust. Team briefs and a periodic newsletter gave information on site development, but fundamental changes in roles and structures are not well communicated. Low trust accounted for much of the poor communication in such a small firm.

While Autopart managers acknowledged the importance of recognition and consistency in their behaviour, these were not guiding models. The role of the 'leading hand' in each of the teams was unclear in the new structure. It seemed as if communication and mutual respect were an afterthought to organizational change, rather than vital to it.

'Teamitis' or time-consuming team activities is often typical of a firefighting culture in transition like Autopart. Team improvement and problem-solving activities tended to have a lower priority than production demands. The manufacturing director did not even find the time to meet the group managers together to discuss the changes, although he realized that this perpetuated their firefighting culture. Design for manufacture was a considerable problem, as there was not sufficient time for testing prototypes in production to eliminate all difficulties. There was little operator/ engineer interface, and less than optimal cooperation, which has added substantially to cost, rework, and reduced lead-times. Operators and supervisors were not customarily consulted about new product lines by the engineers.

The impetus for change at Autopart remained largely reactive to the demands of major clients. Management was characterized as lacking in leadership and tenacity, having too many initiatives and unclear priorities as well as low expectations. In process terms, there was limited proficiency in quality tools, inconsistency in process management and measurement, little follow-through on problem rectification and poor line/engineering interface. In organizational terms, there was poor communication and the lack of a consultative process.

A WORKFORCE UNPREPARED FOR CHANGE

The background to organizational and motivational problems was covered in the two employee attitude surveys. These highlighted that

- Management were perceived to be remote, and uncaring
- Goals and direction were unclear
- Barriers were apparent between operators and management and between departments
- Communication was poor
- Morale was low
- Low trust, 'them and us' persisted

At the conclusion of the quality training, a number of areas requiring improvement were identified by brainstorming, including the lack of management consistency, performance measures not being visible, and the absence of team-performance monitoring. Several things could have improved the situation: the need for a recognition and reward system, the practice of saying 'thank you', and publishing successes. Without these there was very little trust at Autopart.

During the course of research, there was a strike vote on pay issues. Employees felt that management made one excuse after another for keeping wages down: first, low inflation; then, the recession. The annual wage negotiation round cut across new forms of joint activity between employees and management.

Sixty per cent of people in Autopart felt that they lacked the information needed to improve quality, compared to the global survey population of 25%; 80% felt that 'top management talked about quality but did little about it'; 90% felt management cared only about output; 65% of employees felt that performance improvement suffered because of poor feedback, lack of understanding of quality techniques and lack of interest in fellow workers. Autopart employees identified major problems of communication in the company and recommended more information be provided in an open and honest manner.

In a brainstorming session in the quality programme, Autopart employees said that they wanted the following things improved:

- A more open and honest approach (too secretive at present)
- Talking to people directly

- Correct up-to-date information
- More information on how each department worked to be circulated together with an explanation of how departments might link together
- A clear account of profit and loss
- More involvement in situations rather than 'passing the buck'.

Employees felt they had too little information on performance/problems, not enough questions were asked, no notice taken of answers if and when given, and a lack of confidence. They looked forward to more friendliness, more honesty, more courtesy, 'talking to people, not at them' and the eradication of rumours and confrontational barriers.

In general terms they concluded their concerns as follows: the need for consistency and persistency in any initiative, the need for personnel management skills, more trust, better individual treatment of workers and more latitude for cell managers to experiment.

ANTI-ROLLBAR CELL – A FAILED INITIATIVE

Background

This line team was a pilot experience which went badly wrong. The principal problem was the lack of clear and definite boundaries of authority for the cell. The engineer initiating the project promised people too much in terms of self-management, which the works manager could not accept. There was an element of 'not invented here' among senior management, but that was only symptomatic of more fundamental misunderstandings.

In an initial presentation to the board, linking cell manufacturing to world-class performance, an engineer who presented the project was enthusiastic (along with several of his colleagues) about the possibilities of workforce involvement. Employees in the proposed cell were shown a film, indicating to them that if they finished their work, they would be able to organize their own time. While in principle correct (known as a *kanban* manufacturing scheme), the prevailing low trust in the organization, and management's need to maintain control, were strong counterforces.

Objectives

The initial layout of the cell was designed with the participation of all cell members. Training requirements were identified. With hindsight, the supervisor felt that they had erred in going for 'strikers', as the experience would have benefited from a more balanced team. The pilot site was physically isolated, which at the start was good, but as things began to go wrong, it became an added problem.

The cell identified problems in current production to be:

- Long lead-times
- Poor delivery record
- Large inventory
- Excessive paperwork
- Wasted time
- Large indirect staff
- Complicated production control
- Excessive rejects.

The new system proposed 'ownership' of

- Product
- Plant
- Customer requirements
- Tooling
- Planned maintenance
- People resources
- Material stock
- Continuous improvements
- Product quality
- Material planning
- Control systems.

It recommended shorter flow-through routes based on simplification, the removal of job demarcation, and the introduction of skills development. The main benefits were reduced costs based on reduced inventory and rejects. This was achieved by small-batch production based on flexibility. Projected savings on rejects was 32%. Considerable performance achievements were attained, which fell away dramatically when the pilot experience foundered.

Productivity and redundancy

During the initial phase, the pilot cell gained 50% productivity improvement: 'We passed goals more easily than we had anticipated' according to the cell leader. Owing to multiple misunderstandings, performance began to fall off within a year of the start of the experiment. The motivation among shopfloor people was so high in the early days that even the night-shift operators would come in for meetings at the end of the day. Operators were flexible on all machines. As productivity increased, two jobs were eliminated. Redundancies were made because management claimed that the cell was overmanned.

The 'reward' for increased productivity – achieved through the enthusiasm and hard work of the team – was to see two colleagues fired. In retrospect, operators claimed not to have had a clear picture of the quality targets. Some people, they felt, were fired for not achieving targets they did not fully understand:

> One of us was very good at productivity, and generated a lot of rejects. Another worked slowly and had no rejects. We did not know which was the norm.
>
> We were told it would be a different way of working; that we would just be making what we needed; but when we increased production, they just wanted more and more.

Management exert control

The works manager ordered a study on labour input in the area after the pilot cell was launched, intending to demonstrate that it was over-manned. He felt the output of the cell had been taken out of his hands, although he was still responsible for overall profitability. Those involved in the experience pointed to the dramatic quality and productivity gains which were made but were never acknowledged by the manager of manufacturing. He did, however, recognize the successes of the teamwork and ownership. He felt that the pilot experience failed because of mismanagement in setting up the cell. People were told things about increased pay and autonomy which were not delivered. He felt that recognition was given for minimal performance improvement, while it could have been capital spend which improved things.

The conflict of views which resulted in a withdrawal of management support were:

> *Works manager*: I watched it 'from outside'. There was total misapprehension. I was not anti-cell.
> *Supervisor*: Operators were proud but we gave them too much rope too quickly. Senior managers were always critical; never acknowledged the achievements.
> *Initiator of the Cell experiment*: The company wasn't flexible; couldn't absorb it. It backfired.

Peer pressure

Ironically, the final blow to the anti-rollbar cell was peer pressure. If bonuses were to be awarded for productivity, the union wanted them for all employees on the shopfloor, not just the highly productive anti-rollbar cell. There were jealousies about the separateness and difference of the cell among fellow workers. The attempted introduction of operator maintenance responsibilities in the cell was opposed by the unions, regarding it as extra work for not much extra pay. The engineers (who were traditionally responsible for maintenance) could see their jobs being eroded, so their unions got together with the shopfloor unions and opposed the changes. This effectively 'pulled the plug' on the experiment.

Symbolizing the low trust which prevailed at this time, operators asked for flexible tea breaks, which were denied by the works manager. As the opposition mounted from all quarters, the initiator of the experiment reflected:

We didn't have a chance to celebrate our success; peers were jealous and unions were hostile. Senior management feared that they were losing control. In the end, none of us was rewarded. We proved what could be achieved, but the operators asked themselves the question about why they got involved at all.

METAL PREP TEAM – A PARTIAL SUCCESS STORY

Background

The metal prep team was regarded as successful at least by the managing director, who called it 'a correctly structured approach to problems and getting things done'. One of its founder members summarized its purpose as follows:

> This team was set up to improve the paint shop from a need that arose from past frustrations with equipment, and no one addressing the problem for several years.

The project was initiated by good cross-functional participation, including a production engineer, line supervisor and toolroom supervisor and two leading hands, representing the operators. The team began its performance-improvement activities the month following the completion of quality training. Some of the process problems addressed by the team had existed for ten years, but their resolution always took second place to firefighting production problems.

Objectives

One of the major problems was that paint jigs were designed and supplied by the design department without any operator involvement or consultation. Until the team was formed, jigs were tested without consultation from operators on the front line. They sometimes performed poorly in production for two principal reasons: insufficient test and poor communication. The design representative on the team said 'I never heard about the problems. Now I consult directly with the operators for whose station they are made.'

In the course of its activities the team was reported to have evolved into a highly efficient unit with every member contributing freely and acting on tasks set to them. This resulted in the development of pride in the process, and good-natured competition for the completion of tasks. Leadership and drive were essential to the team's success. The production engineers who led the team commented that the problems were much easier to resolve than had been anticipated, once they were given the time and consideration.

After five months' work, sixty improvements had been made. Among the most important were enhancing machine versatility, saving considerable operator time, and eliminating overtime. According to the final report by the team leader, the team demonstrated team spirit, involvement, improved working practices, improved discipline and increased safety awareness.

Employee involvement

Since the team had operator representation only through the leading hands, there was some ill feeling about those 'in and out' of the experience. Briefings to the remainder of the work group were informal, done individually by a supervisor or leading hand. Operators contributed a number of ideas, and prodded the leading hands to get them solved or monitor progress.

One of the achievements was a reduction in overtime, which was a considerable savings to the firm, but the people who gave the ideas lost income. Some said they didn't mind because of the reduction in daily work frustrations. Others said 'We were the fools. We gave ideas to have our wage packets cut.'

Outcome

Working for five months, the team generated an estimated savings of £250 000. Problems such as unnecessary tool changes and bottlenecks had a successful knock-on effect in other parts of the plant. Relations with management were much more collaborative than in the anti-rollbar cell. Cell leaders had direct access to the manufacturing manager and the MD.

While the metal prep team illustrated an excellent example of new operator/engineer or design/production interface, there was a significant downside for employee earning potential. Autopart management was trying to improve performance with new structures, training and the creation of a 'new deal' with the workforce, but in fact, management demonstrated low trust and the culture remained largely unchanged. It did not provide the necessary receptors for the performance improvement initiatives and slowed down the process of change.

Poor Communication and Low Trust at The Engineering Company

8

BUILDING FROM A LOW TRUST BASE

The problems at The Engineering Company were the lack of a time frame for change, and no impetus for change. Communication was poor as people found out about major events from newspapers. Quality was not driven or connected to the basic values of the firm. The quality workshops failed to be embedded in an unchanged hierarchical system. Supervisors were felt to be autocratic by front-line workers and there was cynicism about senior management who seemed to have sudden enthusiasms which were not carried through. The quality programme made little impact on the culture of the organization and the effort was hampered by persistent blame. The Engineering Company was a low trust organization with a blame culture that was difficult to shift.

The firm developed engineering systems for marine navigation and aviation and traditionally held a great many profitable long-term defence contracts with the government. Consequently, The Engineering Company had laborious processes and paperwork, partly explained by defence requirements. The new quality structure became an additive to this bureaucratic system.

Shopfloor teams easily identified numerous frustrations with processes which could not be altered without heavy signature and paperwork requirements. These restrictions had a substantial effect on the prospect for involving people in continuous improvement. It was unclear to employee participants in performance improvement how many of these difficulties were necessitated by customer contract, and how many had just become 'the way things were done around here'. Production managers seemed to have little authority to alter the work procedures or supplies which affected their people, providing at least three layers of frustration.

At the beginning of the cascade of quality awareness throughout the organisation, the managing director's quality improvement team issued a statement reaffirming the quality strategy. It drew attention to the need to obtain the 'active support of our employees and suppliers' in pursuance of the mission. Management committed the company and its employees to continuous improvement.

Major goals included cost savings, delivery performance and customer awareness. The cost of quality in The Engineering Company was calculated at 27% when the process began, on the basis of three categories of charge: (1) test, inspection, qualification testing, documentation; (2) training, supervision and administration, communication meetings, absences; (3) scrap, repeat testing, rework, warranty repair, defect investigation. The quality improvement system was based on the following:

- Commitment
- Awareness – educate and communicate status
- Results – goals to guide quality improvement
- Organisation – meeting unit structure and facilities
- Planning
- Accountability – target setting and progress measurement
- Recognition
- Renewal – reviewing and revising based on experience.

A senior manager in the general manager's quality improvement team was notionally given responsibility for each of these components. In the actual implementation of the quality improvement system or QIS, there were problems with each of these.

PERCEIVED PROBLEMS

A survey following the pilot quality improvement training revealed a set of interesting problems, which reflected issues intrinsic to the culture of

The Engineering Company. Particular problems identified were a lack of feedback on the standard of work, little recognition of 'a job well done' and poor information from managers on quality.

The inadequacy of communication was identified as the most important problem, followed by too much attention to production, not enough to quality, lack of encouragement and lack of team briefings. Respondents felt that managers were rarely around or interested and that more teamwork and time for discussion was needed.

Some direct quotations were additionally revealing:

> Feedback from whom?
> Less time spent 'covering backs' would cause improvement.
> The lack of encouragement affects morale and eventually quality.
> Listening to the views of workers would improve the quality standard.

QUALITY AWARENESS TRAINING

Initial management training was performed by a group of consultants who wrote all the manuals used for the training and distributed to all employees. The training was both cross-divisional and multi-grade. The different disciplines and departmental mix was good, creating greater upstream and downstream understanding of problems.

There was, however, very poor communication about the course to the workforce beforehand, and major fears about the lack of ongoing commitment of management, once people had attended. Rumours were rife that the training involved testing and assessment, generating fear about attending the course. Many had never been asked to attend meetings before (except in their immediate working group) and had certainly never been exposed to this new kind of training.

Some manual workers who were not accustomed to paperwork found it difficult to relate to the abstract tools and concepts. 'For them, this workshop was far from instructive or inspirational; it was a bit of a demotivator as it was over their heads. The danger was to have made 'a large and important section of the workforce insecure about their competence to participate effectively in quality improvement,' according to a course assessor. Each course was opened by a senior manager and closed with a question period by the same. Participants had their worst anticipations confirmed by some poor performances. The reaction to senior management participation was mistrust and cynicism.

From feedback data over the two-year period of the course, it was obvious that most of the participants reacted favourably to the initial experience, relating positively to quality as an important concept at work and a priority for competitiveness. For the majority of employees, it was the first time this type of training had been available to them. For some, it seemed to enhance their personal standing because they were participating with people senior to themselves. A branch secretary of the local union wrote to say that 'the course was an excellent educational experience'.

MANAGEMENT ENTHUSIASMS

Supervisors were described as 'autocratic, facing the culture shock of democratic participation'. Participants expressed fear of criticizing a domineering leader. 'Make us believe that the fear factor will be removed, as until it is, we will not be able to use the system.' Participants asked: 'How will we cope with a manager who is thwarting the progress of quality improvement meetings?' One commented 'my manager thinks that every suggestion is a criticism. How do we achieve a totally open relationship with our supervisors (who may be sensitive to any suggestion that they are not doing everything perfectly) and supervisees, who are reluctant to upset the person doing their annual review?' There was also a persistent belief that senior management commitment on-site was less than wholehearted.

Management were seen by the workforce to have a succession of sudden enthusiasms for panaceas of one kind or another, each of which had a spurt of energy devoted to it, but which flagged as it was succeeded by the next one. 'Quality was very important to the firm, but senior management had a collective expectation of quick results.' 'We never saw senior management. Why don't they talk to us, rather than try to communicate through a remote communication system once in a while?'

Many people felt that more effective communication was critical: 'Downward communication of successes achieved would improve morale, motivation and confidence.' Team briefs were examples of initiatives which were not carried through by the first line of management. 'The core team brief is just handed out with no comment and nothing added.' People wondered if the present enthusiasm would continue, and how it related to daily business demands. They asked:

- 'What is the company's policy on recognition?'
- 'How will we be recognized for our efforts?'
- 'What are the incentives to succeed, financial or otherwise?'
- 'Is the course intended to boost morale?' 'The programme was rolled out in the climate of redundancy and restructuring. Morale was very low.'

'People had been enthusiastic,' according to the senior manager coordinating the programme. But he warned about 'the difficulties of changing deeply ingrained cultural factors in the company, and the danger that these presented for the possibility of change and the effectiveness of the training.' He pointed out that

> having spent considerable time and money making the workforce aware of what we were trying to do, will current management behaviour support or thwart this? Our culture was a fundamental inhibitor to success. It was difficult to persuade people to take more interest without a fundamental management change. No one had recognized the need to change attitudes.

He concluded with a warning from a training assessment feedback questionnaire: 'Managers are still treating their staff as if they were incapable of thought.'

QUALITY IMPLEMENTATION

Some of the teams ran successfully. Others quit because of production demands. Half of the improvement teams in production failed to meet for the usual reasons: – output drive taking precedence and lack of recognition of the importance of quality.

TEAMWORK ASSESSMENT OF PRODUCTION TEAMS

The machine shop

The machine shop with 200 employees served all divisions, and outside customers. Of all the areas in the company, it was seen as a model for potential workforce flexibility, having already developed substantial multi-skilling and flexible teams. At the start of the 1990s, the machine shop lost about 50% of its staff, reflecting the move from specialist to more flexible activities. It began trading with each division on a fixed-price basis, making the mechanical components for all manufacturing systems. Planning and production control had been established with these arrangements.

The machine shop manager felt that the documentation and terminology were onerous, particularly the central reporting, and the handling of the communication and referral. One of the problems he identified was the rotating shift pattern in the machine shop, making people less available for meetings. To facilitate communication between shifts, he suggested the use of specific forms. While an acceptable solution, this slightly defeated the promise of teamwork.

Giro platforms

This was a fairly traditional area of production. The improvement team stagnated after the first few meetings. Members had complaints about the system not dealing with the problems which had been referred upwards. Despite the best efforts of the supervisor, the meeting degenerated into a complaints session. The agenda of the meeting got lost. There is very little structure to it. The supervisor tended to agree about the communication issues and the lack of feedback being a demotivator.

Commissioning and test

This was the most successful team in The Engineering Company. It was well led, with structures in place for feedback. There was an excellent mechanism for reporting problems, for analysis and write-up by front-line supervisors. There was drive and pace to meetings. Test people had higher grade and skill, but the key differentiator of successful teamwork seemed to be the leadership of the local supervisor. The supervisor said that 'Initially people used the improvement team for their own gripes. Since they had no vehicle previously, perhaps it was necessary to clear the ground. It became a bit tiresome. We had to help people understand the benefits of the system.'

Having identified what production problems were, 'people had to think on their feet more, and have a greater understanding of production'. They spent a good deal of time looking at internal customer problems, as the cross-functional consultative structures were not set up. Many of the problems were trivial. Production processes were analysed by the team. Operators were encouraged to communicate with customers for clarification. 'We have sought to make the people realize that quality was not just an engineering issue, that it concerned us all. We have now moved from insignificant to real problems.'

Design engineering

Improvement activity in design engineering was universally recognized to be a failure. The team was an amalgam of two groups working separately. This created morale and motivation problems. There was too much fire-fighting and troubleshooting in the improvement process. The group was too big and too diverse to do effective problem solving. It was difficult to focus on defects; only insignificant problems were raised. Team members felt the identification of defects to be a form of self-inspection – 'pointing the blame at them'. There was little focus because they tried to cover two diverse technologies. The scope of activity was too large and not functionally cohesive. The products also have a differing customer base. Blame for poor performance tended to focus on named individuals in the group. After brainstorming, nothing happened: 'We weren't honest about our priorities. There is low credibility of management ideas: total design, suggestion scheme, appraisal, and communication – nothing seems to work. Is this new team process something else like this?'

Another design engineering team's improvement efforts were more effective largely because the team was made up of a range of engineering functions covering the whole product, including design, control, inspection, test, build, and despatch. It was also a natural team of engineers, working with a single operator. The chair of the team rotated, even to the operator, who was reluctant at first, because he was inexperienced. But he did it, with the encouragement of the supervisor. The bureaucracy remained intact, however: to get the operator to be allowed to function as a rapporteur, the team supervisor had to make a written request on each occasion to the cost centre where he worked.

Inadequate information was one of the first problems addressed, particularly the drawings that were provided to operators. It seemed to take a lot of time to identify then work out problems. The slow progress was a bit discouraging: 'In the quality training, the trainers were good and left us with an enthusiastic approach to getting involved. Now we are perhaps more aware of the time it takes. We are still looking at day-to-day problems, like procedures, which are not in place, but we have created general quality awareness. When we began, we identified 83 potential defects. When we finished reviewing these, we set up defect logs.' The principal issues for the improvement process were product defects, inadequate information and efficiency.

Teamwork problems generally led to poor results because of low trust and lack of recognition for effort. Problems were poor understanding and learning, poor leadership and teamwork and poor management support and feedback. People did not like being taken from the line for meetings, considering them a waste of time.

POOR COMMUNICATION AFFECTS COMMITMENT

Satisfaction with participation in the process had an impact on both motivation and morale. Lateral communication with other departments developed slowly. There was an increasing awareness of problems and costs. Middle management teams usually obtained access to new forms of information. There was also a marked reduction in confrontation. Taking the company seriously helped to build common goals throughout the organization.

Impediments to developing quality were the lack of recognition and cultural problems. In such a low trust environment, employees felt that they were being 'milked again' without any thanks for what they had done. It was not part of the culture to say 'a job well done'. People only heard from their managers when they complained about the work or when there were problems.

The single most important problem throughout The Engineering Company was the absence of effective communication. Progress had been made in formal procedures such as team briefs or newsletters, but the fundamental (informal and pervasive) channels of communication were absent. There was some evidence that the bigger or more difficult the issue, the less well it would be communicated.

The Engineering Company had a pronounced blame culture. Except on an individual basis, very little common ground had been built between management and employees, a 'them and us' culture prevailed. Trying to build common ground proved very difficult, when supervisors and middle managers have very little information and very little that they can deliver in order to reduce major frustrations. As one pointed out: 'Everything is set in stone. Everyone is in the dark.'

Given this situation a rather remarkable beginning was made in certain areas, however tentative. Some teams had partial success, however limited knowledge of the tools and procedures seemed to be. Those teams that seemed to work best were based on employees of a higher technical or professional grade with well-organized and driving leadership.

A young manager working on an MBA thesis on The Engineering Company found a very political atmosphere, a task- rather than people-centred management style, a bureaucratic working atmosphere and short-termism. He found that two thirds of the managers interviewed 'demonstrated varying degrees of arrogance and complacency', evidence of their cynical attitude to customers. Some of the problems identified with quality were the heavily bureaucratic nature of the organization and the 'bolt-on' of the improvement process. The new process became additive to the way work was done, and did not change things fundamentally (Mark Nesbitt, *The Culture in Relation to TQM*, MA thesis, Herriot Watt University, 1993).

Several specific instances of poor communication became apparent during research. All these cut across attempts to gain support for, or commitment to, quality. Some engineers pointed out that they learned of new contracts and new business in the company generally from newspaper reports. Examples of poor communication were plentiful.

In the first instance, the managing director of the firm, who was to have become the deputy chairman, resigned according to the local newspaper. It was assumed on-site that he had been fired because of board discovery of poor pricing on a major contract. This was used as an instance of poor communication, that such an important matter was in the public domain before people were informed internally: 'The Engineering Company was not good at communicating; we operated on fear and rumour. The issue was brought up in several team meetings.'

In the same week a close union vote accepted a pilot scheme to transfer the workforce from a bonus to an appraisal system. This was 'cascaded' down to supervisors in a one-line brief for their teams. People were much better informed by the unions. Employees opposed the scheme vigorously and persuaded many of the inadequately briefed supervisors to join them in these grievances. In this instance some of their most vital people in the communication chain were poorly briefed and vulnerable in putting the management case. A few days later, manufacturing abolished the role of full-time charge hands. Supervisors were briefed on the day that the decision was to take effect. There was no consultation, no warning, and no discussion about how to deal with negative feedback. This change and the manner in which it was done had a negative impact on some of the working teams.

Several supervisors mentioned that they had a two-day course in team brief methods, but they felt that the system had fallen into disrepute: 'Traditional rumour channels were more effective.' This had a significant effect on the credibility of the quality activity. Requests for information to senior management seemed to have been ignored: 'People didn't understand certain things and wanted clarification. My boss could not answer the question either. I suppose it was escalated up, but for months we had no response. When people asked "What about the question which was raised about 4 months ago, the whole system was discredited".'

Another supervisor said that there was a great deal of cynicism about the frequency of company changes and how little these were integrated until the next one was 'cascaded'. The presentation of the team brief in a substantial part of the organization was considered unsuccessful. Supervisors read in a wooden manner the corporate results, which went over most people's heads on the shopfloor. The supervisors were supposed to add a local brief, but it was estimated that half of them did not bother.

The Newsflash, to make spot announcements to employees without calling a formal team brief, was set up to provide information quickly throughout the company by photocopying it and giving it to each individual. Based on a system of 'nodes', it was intended to take four hours to reach everyone in the firm. But senior management found problems in writing the same text for all, to make certain that the words would not be misunderstood. It was very laborious. After several major misunderstandings, it was abandoned.

COMPROMISING CHANGE

The workforce had been a closed shop, based on piecework and bonus schemes. A major step towards harmonization of conditions was initiated in the late 1980s with changes in grades and staff structures. It was extended to include alteration in hours and conditions for shopfloor employees in 1991, reducing hourly paid staff. Appraisals for shopfloor staff were then introduced as part of a package which put an end to the bonus system gradually over two years. The scheme was initially opposed by the unions; they saw it as a loss of power. Time clocks were removed, and the only remaining overtime premiums were paid to the night shift. A career structure was to be established for shopfloor employees.

In The Engineering Company the transfer from bonus to appraisal raised substantial questions for the level of trust which had been able to be built based on potential common interests with management. The transformation of the bonus to appraisal system for the company was a benchmark in the change processes. Incorporation into an appraisal system was a significant opportunity to examine how the culture was functioning and how much actual support (internalized rather than political) there was for the changes. Badly handled, the transformation from a bonus to appraisal system would generate an 'undertow' of bad faith which would remain powerful for years.

In technical and organization terms The Engineering Company was very opaque. Driving process or efficiency change was very difficult in a defence environment. The process 'loops' which directly affected quality through inspection, test and fault reporting were not seriously counted. Strategic priorities were not necessarily clear, except perhaps the drive for lead-time. The time frame for organizational change in a more commercial environment, the imperatives of speed and market response would dictate quicker action. Driving changes for new procedures completely lacked dynamism.

Low trust was evident in the one-day strikes in reaction to the new performance-related pay arrangements. Senior management might have been committed to change, but it was easily scuppered from below. After six months the quality improvement process petered out – through lack of drive, support and lack of performance measurement. There was little customer demand for the transparency of processes. Long lead-times and long design cycles made cost and time variable commodities. Perhaps the greatest accomplishment was considerable fledgling activity in improvement teams, despite the lack of organizational integration and cultural support or consistent process measurement, review and feedback.

Organizational rigidity and bureaucracy were not questioned. Even new procedures were unnecessarily complicated. The traditional defence engineering culture brought with it a system of procedures for procedures' sake, and labyrinthine process mechanisms which had never been questioned. This system was perceived as the principal barrier to quality improvement. Cultural barriers included low trust, blame, poor communication, fear, and a persistent 'them and us'.

A Culture That Would Not   9
Change at Aerco

A CALL FOR CHANGE

'I don't want anyone to tell me it can't be done,' said the general manager of Aerco in the early 1990s at a roadshow. His speech began with a video presentation of the situation in the aerospace industry, indicating $4.7 billion losses in 1991, with twenty airlines ceasing trading, and 150 000 jobs lost worldwide. The downturn in defence spending was an important contributory factor. This was followed by a personal presentation to forty employees at a time by the general manager who explained that the firm needed to be innovative and radical. He asked for cooperation to achieve the benchmark and for a new approach to work based on flexibility rather than job demarcation.

A summary of the negative comments made by employees during the discussions at the roadshow events made very little initial impact on management, which only deepened the already low level of management credibility. Business units and cells were felt to be divisive. Management were not involving people, owing to poor communication. Employees had a low assessment of engineering processes and frustrations in production including supply quality and the lack of an apparent customer–supplier relationship. There was a lack of trust and common ground because of a low level of management credibility, poor communication and institutionalized mistrust in the form of the inspection system. Above all, people on the front line felt that there was a lack of clear conception of the way forward, and a culture based on muddling rather than clarity.

In an employee survey only 12% considered morale to be good, partly because of the commercial situation and poor communication apart from the roadshow. People tended to expect bad news and information about people leaving circulated quickly. The masterplan for change in the factory was referred to as a form of manipulation since it was assumed that management 'know more than they are telling'. Half the people held managers in lower esteem than their supervisors. There was no management tradition of 'walking the job'. Communication was considered to be the key to improving current and future attitudes and the preferred means was through the local team brief. They were looking for more information about daily output and opportunities to make suggestions, give ideas and get feedback. They wanted to be involved in problem solving and decision making.

People were looking for leadership and direction from management and their willingness to listen by being open to ideas and suggestions. They were called upon to focus on major problems, not minor issues, and for their capacity to deliver. Employees sought clear roles and authority as well as new skills. They felt that trust was lacking. Better communication was needed – particularly daily information about the job, feedback on performance and updates on the performance of each unit. Employees sought opportunities to make suggestions and give ideas, become involved in problem solving and decision making and in making change work. More evidence of customer–supplier partnerships between the business units was needed as well as a clarification of budget allocation and a reduction in the prevailing blame culture between business units.

A NEW STRATEGY FOR CHANGE

The follow-up to the roadshow discussions led to a series of recommendations on employee involvement in problem-solving, change planning, implementation and decision making. A strategy document released the year following the roadshows identified the changes needed in organizational and cultural terms to support the new competitive aims of Aerco.

It was noted that demarcation on the shopfloor was breaking down, yielding to more flexibility. But too much time was still spent on in-

ternal conflicts, with a perceived need to refocus on external competitors
and environment, and to get people to understand the business issues. It
was believed that new scope for recognition and reward would help to
improve people's outlook. There was a need to replace overtime as 'a way
of life'. Multilevel teamwork was inhibited by demarcation issues, which
needed to be transformed into new forms of flexibility.

Employees felt that the organization was cumbersome and they did not
understand how it functioned. In many cases structures were out of date
and poorly defined. There was a proliferation of narrowly defined jobs;
which needed to be enhanced and redefined. The organization reflected little
potential for the future. There was a lack of resource or succession planning. Management lack of skill was felt to be at the heart of the brake on
the development of the organization. The introduction of cell manufacturing
fragmented the organization into smaller pieces and accentuated problems,
rather then solving them. Cross-cell customer–supplier relationships
remained very fraught. There was little evidence of partnership.

'People in Aerco have a strong work ethic. We need to create an environment to make it work,' said the personnel director. This strong work
ethic was borne out in interviews and observations. Production bottlenecks were perceived to be one of the main frustrations by employees. In
some parts of the plant there was considerable overmanning and idleness.
An experiment proved how much slack could be drawn in by enhancing
productivity per shift. Relations with the unions were described by site
management as good. Loyalty to the site was high. And the business was
vital to the prosperity of the local community.

AN EXPERIMENT IN CHANGE

Aerpart, the components business at Aerco, needed to achieve the most
dramatic change. Traditionally it made parts for the airframe business, its
key customer, which suffered drastically reduced demand, raising a question about its future. Aerpart had to shift from being a supply business to
becoming a stand-alone business with customers from other plants in the
group.

Aerpart made 49 000 parts, in a vast array from advanced computer-controlled machining to handcrafted metal pieces for aircraft assembly. Some of the equipment was up to 50 years old and had been used to press forms of the Lancaster aircraft for the Second World War! Plant maintenance of such a large volume and variety of machining equipment was one of the key problems. Some were maintained in service by the tacit knowledge or 'black arts' of their operators.

Meeting due date delivery by introducing site throughput efficiency had been one of the biggest challenges. Creating an understanding of individual and group responsibility for the throughput process was the purpose of the new project generated with the help of Digital group consultants. The principal problem facing Aerpart was whether or not this new design process would be implemented, or whether it would go the way of other efforts like cell management because of lack of clarity or drive or both. The new model was based on the need to change behaviour and attitudes in the workforce, but whether or not the design team and project participants would be able to generate a shared vision of that change was open to question.

Following years of inspection typical of the aircraft industry, it seemed difficult for quality assessments to be linked to anything but product quality. The institutionalized mistrust created by the inspection culture had been transformed by self-inspection on the shopfloor based on a product certification scheme. There was deep scepticism about quality. Initiatives needed another mantle to achieve credibility. In a presentation to the workforce, the Aerpart business manager identified the criteria for their success as quick response to orders; on-time delivery and securing profitable repeat orders from existing customers as well as new ones. The new design process was intended to address that.

Part of the difficulty was inherent in the culture itself, according to a manager of the change process. This explained why there was so little performance measurement. 'Part of the price which was paid for change,' he volunteered, 'was to introduce some clarity of performance measurement to a culture accustomed to muddling and masking performance by measuring activity only. We are geared up for failing. Firefighting becomes a virtue and lighting fires was occasionally essential to keep the system going'. He declared the business to have a risk-averse blame culture, which needed radical change.

Cell management did not appear to have generated teams which really functioned as cells, despite new demarcations on the factory floor, and name plaques. In the views of some – particularly operators – the cell structure fragmented the business and introduced additional opportunities of blaming other people: 'Everyone tried even harder to stitch everyone up'.

ORGANIZATIONAL CHANGE: THE DESIGN PROCESS

In the United States in the 1980s Digital had some considerable success with high performance work groups, largely self-managed teams. The only location in which HPWGs were used in manufacturing in Europe was in the Ayr plant for a period of three years in the 1980s when a new workstation was being built, in a 'greenfield location', an area of the existing plant which was cleared for the project. The favourable results were well known throughout the Digital Group.

The Digital change process was based on selective participation in the organizational design. It began with the creation of an understanding of the expectations of customers, management, suppliers and employees (called charterers). The purpose, mission, objectives and goals of the organization were developed as a guiding philosophy of values and beliefs. In the early stages of the design process the Aerpart teams discussed all of these.

The objective was to understand that the team must meet the demands of customers. Once team building was completed, the design of the work process was started with new job design and responsibilities. From the design of the teams, the organizational design was expected to emerge in the collectivity. These then were compared with the charterers' expectations and the organizational design was revised. Aerpart employee expectations in the new design process were outlined to include job satisfaction, a fair rate of pay, a safe working environment and job security. It would have been impossible for the firm to deliver on job security.

PROMISE AND DISAPPOINTMENT

The activity which was the most help to the project was the exercise which each of the six design teams undertook to try to establish what makes people work best. Each team was charged with working these ideas through and discussed them at great length, refining them from a brainstorming process. These were outlined in the Introduction to this book.

Other issues which came up in discussion were that operators were never given an opportunity to see their completed work on an aircraft, nor did they know their way around the rest of the factory or what went on there. Awareness of the completed job and the work environment were identified as important. Poor communication was felt to undermine a lot of positive efforts. Operators observed, 'We were trusted to an extent to do the job through the product certification scheme: it gave us pride in our work. But were we really trusted?'

Operators on the shopfloor wanted to be part of the decision process, to have a 'cheque book' for the cell to renew equipment. 'Since tool renewal was allocated to the cell things have improved 100%.' The cell leader said 'We used the tools more carefully – having ownership ensured responsibility. We spent a lot less on tools since it was localized. Having a say in expenditure gave us a sense of achievement. We worked best when we implemented the actions because of the sense of achievement. We wanted to be part of the decision making.'

Only about 10% of the workforce was represented in the new design process. They were selected for participation by supervisors as leaders in a cell team. Many of them were shop stewards. They reported back to the others in a briefing, or informally, the results of each two days of the design process. The sheer ratio of activity of the 'in-team', relative to those who were not part of the process, was indicative that there was an inner and an outer circle, which the design process had created. The tendency for pilot activities on the shopfloor to set themselves off from the rest of the production process had often raised an unfortunate distinction, which could undermine the experiment. There was a commonly held view in the workforce that the masterplan to which the project must work already had a design and that the participants were merely being 'manipulated' by a predetermined plan. This was evidence of how little trust there was at Aerco.

There was very little change in teams or processes, which might have heralded a radical alternative. Cells were not really functioning; performance was very poor, and little enough changed in the way the business had been run for the previous decade. The design team admitted that the process had been very slow, because of the lack of trust or common ground even among participants in the pilot experience. There was little real involvement in a process which was supposed to create ownership. Cell leaders doubted that it was possible to create a shared vision in just two hours a week.

From a fragmented environment, accustomed to blaming others on a regular basis, with no previous common ground, how did one begin to build ownership and commitment? The process did not seem real. With so little actual participation, could a shared vision be effectively communicated to the others? Would it not take very much longer than the time the business had to pull itself around?

People were interested to know when they could participate in designing their own team. The creation of a shared vision in the project team took a rather time-consuming eight days of work, with varying degrees of success. The entire workforce understood the external threat to the business and the need to change. From a common process of building 'buy-in' they were allowed to participate in an already formed vision. At the end of the day, the design process was much more suited to a single project (the new PC in the Digital Ayr plant) with none of the complications of the size and complexity of the Aerco business.

The most successful exercise observed in the Aerco design process was teaching the team to think like a small stand-alone business. The role-playing was excellent. The greatest return was obtained when change was based on the specific processes.

The Aerco management team recognized that something needed to change but there was no real awareness of how to change it. The general manager and some others thought it was a lack of a will to win. Half-way through the nine-week process it became apparent, in an important management team meeting, that there was a great deal of uncertainty about the direction of the pilot effort.

In an assessment carried out at the mid-point in the process of all the members of the design team individually, the recognition of the need for change was clear, but the vision of the future was not shared. This reflected a lack of general understanding of the values, a lack of common vision, and varying degrees of understanding of the potential for improvement. A lack of clear conception in the project was pervasive among the design team (all of whom were trained by Digital consultants).

There were two principal questions for Aerco:

1 Was it this radical departure from the traditional organization and culture which was required to meet performance demands in the coming years?
2 In the process of developing the new model, what might be compromised by the weight of the traditional organization or, more importantly perhaps, its culture?

The design process itself was questionable, since it was a representative experience touching only 10% of the workforce which might raise problems of 'buy-in' to the process in the initial phases of implementation. Aerco had set itself a big challenge, given the sheer size and scale of the redesign and the numbers of people it involved. Most firms which have moved to such a radical change, had already made fairly substantial changes to their organizations and cultures prior to empowering work groups. The success of these change programmes, which focused on self-management, relied on a series of interrelated factors to make a new shared vision of change possible. In Aerco the prospect of reversion in the early stages was quite marked. The problems consisted of little support from the plant executive team, no clear profile for the business and no understanding of the process by outsiders.

PROBLEMS OF OWNERSHIP

The assemblies team

The assemblies team was a pilot cell for performance improvement. Another ten people whose activities impacted on theirs joined the core team of eight. The cell had been a poor performer in throughput, quality and lead-time. The production layout was deemed unsatisfactory, and was one of the first things to be changed. The objective of the project was to get from a 17–27-week lead-time to 48 hours in six weeks. In order to achieve this, controlled sequencing and set-up times were developed. Poor storage and lack of scrap recording was one of the problems generated by constant firefighting to get orders out.

Support activities were centralized to overcome poor throughput performance. Breaking down demarcation, by creating process ownership among operators, led to running and operating cranes or delivering parts to customers on demand. Lesser skilled operators thus gained some variation in their work. While the project never reached its two-day objective, delivery time was reduced substantially. The short-term gains were its main achievement. But the impetus of the project was lost and the performance gradually began to deteriorate. Performance measures were not kept up to date. Once interest was lost, performance began to slip.

Organizational issues

Early on there was serious concern about the operators participating in the group exercise because of lack of support for the process. There was pervasive cynicism and defensiveness. Observation of the team in the design process confirmed these observations; they were a form of 'testing the waters' rather than outright opposition. No-one in the design group seemed willing to talk to people openly about the commonality of the threat to future business. More time was taken up being critical of particular attitudes in the workforce than trying to understand what caused them. Even though there was an outspoken minority, most of the others established some common ground for working. It was not obvious that the design team or the process itself could exploit effectively that newly developed common ground and potential for building trust.

Employee involvement

The cell leader described scepticism among his people, which was based on whether or not their views were genuinely sought, or they were being led through a masterplan of someone else's making. The biggest risk, he felt, was that peoples' expectations would not be fulfilled. It was not entirely clear what these expectations were, except to have a hand in designing the new organization and running it. Although the Digital process was designed as self-management, this was not considered at Aerco. Some of the cell managers felt that there might not be a clear award of responsibility, with a stop–start approach to overall autonomy, which would undermine the process. There was little experience which could prepare operators for self-management, since the cell structure was supervisor-driven. There was nothing else in the culture which would indicate a willingness to change things radically.

Results anticipated

It was clear to the cell manager that the pilot process was not tied to performance measurement. 'It was called a journey, but what was the destination?' The cell manager felt that the key imperatives, such as throughput efficiency and due date delivery, had very little meaning for the operators. They might have regarded themselves as efficient, but had no understanding of the process. The design process was like a course, and the transfer of ownership was neither clear nor related to performance improvement.

The equipping team

The equipping team was another pilot for the Digital design process. All the operators participated in the process, and as they became involved in the relationships between direct and indirect staff became markedly more collaborative. One gain was to promote a clear understanding of the customer among indirect staff.

Outcome

Weekly quality meetings included 85 operators – all the teams in the assembly area. The aim was to create an understanding of what could and what could not be improved in scrap and rework. Business development targets were being adapted for measurement in the cell. These awareness meetings also addressed health and safety issues and personnel matters. Inputs and outputs to each of the teams were simplified, so that operators could understand the throughput bottlenecks and participate in dealing with them. The unions in the cell were quite active in support of these changes. Some of the supervisors created problems by not accepting the need for constant communication.

The cell manager worked on four basic requirements for successful implementation providing leadership and drive for building teamwork, understanding target measurement, skill flexibility and communication. He felt that this would help to overcome low trust and suspicion. He thought that he needed to redress low management credibility, earned by a great deal of talk and less action or demonstrable results.

Creating team spirit was difficult for people who were accustomed to working alone at their bench, and who had never had to work together as a team. Creating ownership of change was also a problem, because operators and supervisors typically expected management to solve problems.

The Defence Company: 10
Structured Change in
Production but Less Commitment

INITIATING ORGANIZATIONAL CHANGE

A mass meeting at The Defence Company in 1989 was a cornerstone of the changes in business strategy, communication, downsizing and re-structuring to be implemented throughout the 1990s. The general manager of this plant, which manufactured military hardware, attempted to define a common challenge to propose radical change in the business. In his presentation he said 'I will be with you outside the factory gates if we do not succeed'. This type of address was heard for the first time at this plant. In a glossy brochure produced for the occasion, the GM promised that 'all personnel would have the opportunity to be involved, to contribute and participate'. The works committee, including union representatives and shop stewards, picked up from his initial presentation and 'ran with it'. According to the manufacturing manager, 'they were reading the change management literature to keep ahead of what we were doing'.

The 'site baronies' of the company, with their 'autocratic style' and hierarchical command control management, were dismantled to make the company more responsive to market demands. The process capability in manufacturing included machining, mechanical fabrication and assembly, electro-mechanical assembly, electronic assembly (printed circuit boards), plating and painting. The most recent products required the procurement of more and more sophisticated sub-systems, with a decline in the proportion of in-house work.

The manufacturing division's major change process began in 1990 (when

75% of production was for the Ministry of Defence). They abandoned all non-missile business and concentrated on their core competence. The workforce declined from 3000 in 1988 to 1300 in 1993. A *Kawasaki* Production System (KPS) was introduced, aiming to create a logical and streamlined workflow. KPS is a low-inventory or 'pull' system of manufacturing linked to *kanban* supply and stocking, and designed to reduce lead-times. As a means of introducing just-in-time manufacturing and continuous improvement, KPS eliminates non-value-added work. It requires education and training, action-centred leadership, multi-skilling and continuous improvement. The real issue lies in the willingness of front-line workers to identify with and internalize practices and procedures in a new production culture. KPS is achieved by an integrated set of initiatives based on clarity, transparency and consistency of task and responsibility. Usually reserved for large-volume production of cars or other consumer items, it was an interesting experiment to introduce KPS into a low-volume batch environment like missile production.

With the assistance of a major consulting firm, the physical organization of the plant was redesigned and restructured to accommodate the KPS. A series of organizational changes flattened the management structure, introduced integrated production teams of engineers and front-line managers located in the manufacturing area. The system promoted defect reviews, and encouraged operator participation in continuous improvement action groups. As a vehicle of change, KPS proved to be an excellent basis on which major organizational and cultural changes could also be built. Driving change through a visible and coherent restructuring process in manufacturing seemed an ideal way to shake up the traditional manufacturing environment.

A fundamental question for the firm was to what extent they have succeeded in changing the culture to support the dramatic changes in production. Cultural changes ultimately proved important to the success of the organizational changes. While people realized that there was a threat to their jobs, little enough common ground was built with management on the idea that the commercial success of The Defence Company was a common goal for all. While management were complimentary and loyal to their men, this is quite different from actually awarding them responsibility for process improvement. Recognition or saying 'a job well done' was not really part of the culture.

The continuous improvement action groups which were initiated were not working for a fairly specific set of reasons:

• Demotivation of manual workers by encouraging them to initiate a problem-solving process without providing the tools to take the process to conclusion
• Designating the groups to be engineer-led, thus reinforcing the difference between front-line and professional staff
• Lack of common working space for the group
• Young and enthusiastic team leaders with an excellent attitude to team members were no substitute for training and experience on the team. There remained an ample reservoir of talent, energy and goodwill which had not been tapped.
• The new structure closed off traditional succession and promotion procedures based on good performance, which was a significant demotivating factor for front-line staff. New team leaders blocked promotion, and despite their enthusiasm they were criticized by team members for not understanding the working processes.

The extent of organizational change achieved in a defence firm with a single major customer was impressive. There was a long tradition of institutionalized mistrust based on inspection. This hampered progress in the new model. A leader who radically altered the operational structure, trimmed the workforce and the way work was undertaken, as well as communicated with people honestly about the business and its future, for the first time generated change. This obviously made an important impact. Combined with the visible, physical and easily understandable changes made through KPS, there were probably important 'receptors of change' in the thinking of most people.

An employee survey in 1990 indicated that 55% of people from all sites of the company were interested in becoming more involved, but this dropped significantly to 39% for the category of manual workers. A favourable rating of the firm as an employer was 58% overall, but 40% for manual workers. Only 22% of manual workers felt that they could do more for the company, and only 24% felt informed about what was going on. Work and job satisfaction were not favourable at the time. Skilled workers wanted more responsibility, but did not welcome new forms of accountability.

While employees felt that their managers were approachable and good communicators, senior management was described as aloof, showing little recognition for the work done by employees. People interviewed were unanimous in their view that management had to become more open, encouraging closer contact with the workforce once the changes had been accomplished. This was improved in part by 'walkabouts'.

The new manufacturing strategy was based on core competence in missile production, in-house manufacture of key components, an overhaul of scheduling and control systems, and a reduction in cost of production, lead-times and inventory levels. A new management team led the strategy while attempting to create a positive, flexible workforce. To create an improvement in performance key areas of quality, processes, facilities and inventory management were targeted. The improvements to be made included the traditional segregation of design and manufacturing, poor production and engineering control, poor materials flow and capacity utilization, significant duplication and the lack of productivity measures. Management had been top-heavy, relying on a lot of indirect staff.

The net result was an unfocused manufacturing function, reduced profitability due to high costs, and extraordinary efforts to meet contract and delivery requirements in a highly complex and wasteful organization. There was a need to eliminate planning chaos, firefighting and waste. The first changes made focused on employee involvement and accountability, including multi-skilled production teams, minimum direct and indirect supervision, and flexible working practices. The leaner flatter manufacturing structure featured few management layers, greater individual responsibility and accountability, product-focused multi-skilled manufacturing cells and new criteria for management selection based on teamworking skills.

EMPLOYEE INVOLVEMENT AND ACCOUNTABILITY

The quality philosophy at the plant emphasized worker involvement. The operating values stated that 'people were our greatest strength. Success in all we do is achieved through involvement and teamwork in an environment which respects the contribution of the individual'. Continuous improvement was to be achieved by 'teamwork ... as the means by which problems were solved, working together in an open and constructive manner with each employee making a personal contribution and supporting the other members of the team'. A number of activities were designed to generate wider employee involvement. These included a leaner manufacturing organization with increased individual accountability; multi-skilled integrated production teams; minimum indirect/direct manning; flexible working practices; and an open management environment. The leaner, flatter manufacturing structure reduced management grades from nine to four and added greater personal responsibility and accountability, the use of psychometric analysis for the first time, and management competence based on teamwork skills and acceptance of change. Flexible working practices were promoted by retraining to remove demarcation and achieve simplified manufacturing methods, harmonization of conditions of employment and product-oriented multi-skilled manufacturing cells.

One rationale for flexible working practice was to generate greater job satisfaction. Reforms were self-financing through productivity agreements. The ultimate goal was to develop a 'can do' culture in manufacturing, emphasizing problem solving, teamworking and continuous improvement. Self-inspection was introduced through a plant-wide product certification scheme. The change was rapid and impressive, particularly for a manufacturing facility with exacting inspection and other procedures.

Quality council management considered what aspects of quality control could be passed to the operations department as part of the new product certification scheme. Quality control liaised with the operations department to formulate rules and procedures, and pilot schemes were initiated. The initial presentation to operators joining the scheme was by already certified supervisors and included a witty DTI-sponsored video on quality, 'Managing into the 1990s'. Supervisors relied on a set of twelve slides prepared for them, but many of them had poor presentation skills. These presentations were essential to the initial acceptance of the scheme. There was resistance to accept the quality control stamps because of the volume of work, and the addition of extra responsibility without extra pay.

Operators were trained on the job by inspectors, and approved after three months of one-to-one training. A thousand operators went through this training. The product certification schemes also added an operator suggestion scheme. Approved operators frequently offered considerable additional information on a fault note. In the early 1990s 95% of operators were certified under the scheme. A detailed monitoring programme for entry to the scheme followed, as did the operation of the scheme in a fully certified phase. Operator product controls indicated the process for repeat checks and error correction. Among the strengths of the scheme were fewer repeat failures and the recognition and partial empowerment of operators. The driver for this scheme was cost savings on the inspection function. The outcome was to ensure that the ownership of product quality was on the shopfloor. The implementation of the scheme was intended to improve material flow and intrinsic quality, remove non-value-added activities and gain a 'right first time' commitment.

PROBLEMS OF MANAGEMENT ATTITUDE

A fundamental question impacting on the success of change was the extent to which management succeeded in changing the culture to support the organizational changes, which had been initiated. Cultural changes were important to achieve some of the objectives required. While people realized that there was a threat to their jobs, little enough common ground was built with management on mutual understanding of the potential commercial success of The Defence Company. A 'hail fellow, well met' management approach typified by 'my men are great,' was quite different from giving them responsibility for process improvement.

In the early 1990s there was a total transformation of senior management. Those who did not fit the new mould were retired. In the changed management structure, support for the team leaders or group managers had still to be built among shopfloor operators, whose traditional respect was based on detailed knowledge of the job and proven skill performance.

At the end of the day, though, the participation of front-line workers was less than satisfactory because little else had changed in the culture, and little common ground developed between engineers and workers in the action groups. Although front-line staff were represented in process improvement groups, they felt themselves to be in an adjunct relationship to engineering staff, unrecognized for their local expertise and without the tools or skills to be effective participants in the process.

A QUESTION OF POOR MORALE?

Human error was largely based on poor morale, according to a KPS audit. But was it just a question of morale? Attention to the type of controls and procedures similar to KPS has been observed in other British factories. It was not only innate to the Japanese worker. The real issues lay in the willingness of the operator to identify with or internalize practices and procedures as 'the way things are done around here'. That could be achieved by an integrated and interlocking set of initiatives based on clarity, transparency, and consistency of task and authority. It needed to be based on a recognition and respect for the local expertise of each worker, encouraging him or her to make continuous improvement part of all tasks.

The continuous improvement action groups set up in 1993 did not work because the operators needed to get together with engineers to identify problems. The group manager found that there was no occupational or professional liaison, no common understanding of the ground rules, and no common playing field between shopfloor people and higher technical grades. The operators at the initial meetings suggested ideas and were told, for example, that these suggestions were 'non-conforming with quality procedures, not in the design, not up to engineering standards, or too costly'. The process soon fell into disrepute with the shopfloor people, who were reported to have been relieved when the group manager suspended it. 'People on the shopfloor want to know everything: they were protecting their jobs like there was no tomorrow,' said one of the managers. Operators were an important part of problems solving. When the continuous improvement action groups were suspended, the operators retained regular access to engineers, and escalated the problem to team leaders if necessary: 'They certainly didn't like sitting around the table and getting nothing done,' said the product manager.

An improvement team was also set up to consider defects by reducing yield to test, and changeover times. 'We had to build confidence initially,' said the group convenor, 'because people had been on teams before and nothing had happened. They felt sceptical understandably. We had to convince them that this time it would be different.' He felt that an early 'quick win', with a particular form of testing equipment, would be essential to show them, but there was some doubt as to whether there was sufficient funding for this. 'People don't feel personally blamed any longer for defects. The product certification scheme moved us on from that. But operators had learned to live with problems which were typically not analysed and rectified,' according to the convenor.

The Defence Company introduced performance-related pay in the mid-1990s for manual workers in order to support the team performance. There was a gainshare scheme based on the quality and delivery performance. There remained a discrepancy between the aims of the culture change at The Defence Company and the reality of effective opportunities for worker participation. An excellent start had been made in the context of the restructuring for KPS. But the company still had the feel of a 'them and us' culture, with little genuine commitment from the workforce. In many instances operators were temporary or marginal participants indicative of how little common ground had yet been developed.

Part III

Chapter 11 is a radical departure from the case material presented in Part II. It looks at the prospect for change in some of the leading global investment banks. This chapter is an extension of the major argument of the book on trust to a different sector. The argument focuses on the value which collaboration can bring to institutions currently dominated by a star system and high individual reward. Investment banks operate in a highly competitive and risky environment, only partly offset by building increasingly larger institutions in the 1990s. Capital ratings may not be the only measure of success in the future. Two new forms of capital – social capital and client loyalty – offer new opportunities. Beyond the current era of star players, a knowledge edge may create a new generation of bankers fascinated by the potential of working with colleagues to develop outstanding integrated products and services – mining collaborative intelligence and interpretation. Changes in organization, culture and the time allocated to long-term collaborative assets can transform investment banking. The first step, though, will prove the hardest – to focus the attention of senior management away from deal making and short-term results towards longer-term transformation, which may in time reap bigger and more secure rewards.

The final chapter of the book considers what it takes to become a trusted leader. Using many of the concepts developed in Part I, the chapter focuses on the interpersonal skills needed by today's leaders in business if they are to build commitment in the workforce. Leaders in this new era of business are called upon to earn authority without control. Economic and social changes have generated new demands for management by consent rather than control. People today are looking for more than a low trust organization as a place to work. Trust is a key ingredient in successful leadership. Loyalty and paternalism are a thing of the past, no longer suitable for the demands of business today. The leader is the guardian of the corporate values and strategy. Successful leaders become the storykeepers and storytellers of the vision and values of the firm.

Trust can release the energy of people and enlarge the scope of human and intellectual capital in a firm by encouraging people to give more of themselves and build commitment to strategic goals. Chapter 12 returns to several of the general themes for building trust for competitive advantage. Successful wealth creation and the opportunity to become an industry leader cannot be based only on the strategy and innovation of senior management. It relies on changing the way the organization thinks and operates. Trust needs to be built into the strategy and systems at the core of a successful company if the mobilization and maximization of resources is to be achieved.

Collaborative Capital and Client Loyalty in Investment Banks   11

BEYOND CAPITAL RATINGS

Capital ratings may not be the only measure of success for investment banks at the start of the new century. Two new forms of capital – social capital and client loyalty – offer the opportunity to make significant changes in the way business is conducted. Social capital is the value created by collaboration, not simply individual talent and performance. Beyond the current era of star players, the knowledge edge of competition may create a new generation of bankers fascinated by the potential of working with colleagues to develop outstanding integrated products and services – mining collaborative intelligence and interpretation. If price and speed of quote have been the traditional vectors of competition, future value for customers is likely to be based on more integrated products and customized services. But investment banks are a long way from being structured, or their people motivated and rewarded, to take advantage of such opportunities.

At the end of a decade of the creation of mega-institutions with global reach, there is a future in mining the internal sources of capital which have come together through agglomeration, but have not yet realized their potential value. Changes in organization, culture and the time allocated to long-term collaborative assets will transform investment banking. The first step, though, will prove the hardest – to focus the attention of senior management from deal making and short-term results to longer-term transformation which will in time reap bigger and more secure rewards.

Most of the last decade has been taken up with building increasingly larger global institutions in the race to be one of the major players. And much senior management time has been absorbed by digesting diverse institutions, product lines, expertise, cultures and board members. Size is intended to counter market volatility and risk by creating a complex array of products. Cross-subsidy balanced the losses of particular product lines brought on by commoditization and eroding margins. For some products, the economics were clearly unsustainable, as the cost of doing business rose above the cut price of intermediation – accelerated by the growth of on-line trading. Price and speed of quote became the pivotal terms of competition. As price competition became more and more acute, it left some corporate clients wondering if the banks might eventually take a longer-term view of their own requirements and volatile business trends. Instead, clients typically faced a wide array of products – very often being sold by different parts of the same firm.

Goldman Sachs, Morgan Stanley and J. P. Morgan have excellent track records with key clients, most of which are deeply personalized and based on long-term association and relationship building. They are aggressive, sometimes ruthless at winning new business, but take a long-term holistic view of clients once won. Goldmans built initial relationships by saving clients from predators decades ago, and began a tradition of taking a stake in new client issues or other forms of expansion. Their close relationships with clients gave them access to proprietary information which enabled them to generate tailored products and services earning a premium.[1] Most banks try to practise this in one form or another. Universal banks, such as Deutsche and ABN Amro, with both investment and commercial/corporate banking, have introduced a senior banker role to take charge of key corporate relationships. Senior bankers convey a personal veneer over a complex set of fragmented product lines, sometimes bypassed by other mechanisms such as 'fast-tracking' for particular institutions. As yet there is little enough activity which has crossed the lines of investment and corporate banking, apart from some spectacular corporate finance deals. An overlap of expertise and activity is becoming common – investment banks have been moving into syndicated and structured lending, and corporate banks into loan securitization. Yet a convergence of products does not necessarily generate broader collaboration unless some major effort is made. The corporate departments of commercial banks have, of course, less product diversity and fragmentation, and much longer product cycles. The whole pace of business and relationships is different. The potential collaboration with investment banking colleagues is added value yet to be exploited.

Most of today's successful Europe-wide deals are still based on personal network leverage on behalf of a client, which will increase business incrementally but not yet in a sustained fashion. Research capability is often dispersed and vital information is simply not shared. Much more could be done while preserving the Chinese walls essential for compliance. The growth in client relationships should never interfere with the vital sharpness of analysts' independent advice (a recent concern in the City and on Wall Street). Collaboration while maintaining well-marked boundaries can be very effective. The fragmentation of sales, for example, is often driven by client protection – jealously guarded relationships – rather than opening up on a reciprocal basis to a full range of information and support across borders. Institutions are struggling to continue to integrate their components in Europe – reluctant to lose local market share (and often brand capability) in the home market for the secondary goal of cross-European integrated sales. The push for quarterly results and bonus pools naturally reinforces this. Colleagues in London or Madrid simply do not have the time or incentive to deal with the portfolio placements of Italian clients, for example. Cross-border activity, despite the projections, seems still to be personal, haphazard and difficult, largely because reward structures have not been significantly altered.

Until now, senior management have been pre-occupied with agglomeration and system development so the component parts of the businesses could at least communicate. This allowed scant time to consider some of the bigger issues – the balance between short- and long-term goals, the reward and remuneration system or the other mechanics, all of which could generate new value. As these issues are more fundamental and complex – difficult and messy – since they involve people and cultures, they are often put off. The real challenge in the coming years lies in the capacity to make major changes in the way business is conducted, moving towards higher levels of integration internally and the capacity to be more responsive with ideas and opportunities for clients.

Banks have developed strategic plans and policies, but implementation of these new ideas or the creation of real future value from potential integration is yet to come. The sheer effort to tie together diverse institutions has kept strategy formulation in the major institutions focused on products, national consolidation or international reach. Internal transformation has been concerned with trying to knit together diverse businesses and cultures, making rationalizations of staff and deciding which of senior management will join the board. These changes have been (understandably) disruptive and time-consuming, especially trying to pull together sometimes different cultures (Morgan Stanley Dean Witter, for example, or more recently Deutche Bank and Bankers Trust). Implementation will take longer, in the course of which a new form of leadership potential may be developed. There are probably more mergers to come alongside European growth which will perhaps place these changes on a longer agenda once again. The broader product base and cross-subsidy of different product lines is central to the strategy of increasingly larger institutions. In the good years, this strategy has offered excellent returns.

RISK AND TRUST

Operational risk – or the potential loss from the breakdown of controls on people and systems – is even more difficult to control than market risk. The big earners with star salaries give little heed to management, let alone 'bean counters' (internal auditors and accountants). While millions have been spent on regulatory compliance, following the Barings debacle, most institutions still control operational risks sketchily at best. Any driven and determined employee can get around the controls, willing to invent new evasions if the price is right. The bonus system becomes, in effect, a form of option with no risk of having to even out performance earnings with the firm in bad years (something Salomon Smith Barney mooted a few years ago, but – not surprisingly – failed to introduce). It is ultimately impossible to control high earners for whom the downside risk is merely losing a job, compared with a tremendously lucrative upside. Some would argue that the psychology of these 'masters of the universe' makes them see risk totally differently from lesser mortals like senior managers or the rest of us.

Established status puts traders and analysts out of reach of conventional management. This feature of internal status and organization impacts dramatically on the opportunity to control risk. Even Goldman Sachs, with a powerful partnership culture and high levels of integration, could not keep control of risky decisions taken in both Italy and the UK in 1994 which threatened their profitability. Product specialists in Goldman Sachs had always been encouraged to take risks, with a wide latitude of accountability. It did not work. From a broadly accepted culture of diffused responsibility, they had to consider much tighter controls, especially as they were growing very rapidly outside the United States at that time.

In some investment banks, the bonus round ties up output and emotional energy for up to eight weeks in each annual cycle. It resembles the annual wage round in manufacturing in the USA in the 1970s and the UK in the 1980s, when firms subjected themselves to a yearly ritual which was both distracting and potentially damaging to morale and relationships. Senior management in investment banks clings to the idea that the only way to reward people is through compensation. Commercial banks have less of a problem with stars. The earnings differential is much less great, specific expertise is not so esoteric, and there is much more attention to career development. But the mercenary and fiercely competitive culture of investment banks masks a host of other opportunities for demonstrating how to value people. Future profitability and outstanding performance on innovation lie in reconsidering these practices, which most bank executives continue to believe are immutable.

Investment banks operate in a very risky environment – only partly offset by agglomeration and a broader array of products. But they have not yet entirely managed to overcome operational risk. Shareholders who are less and less sanguine about market risks in different parts of the world take an even dimmer view of the destruction of shareholder value by operational risk and the continual escalation of costs, particularly in equities and fund management. Many of the major players have clarified their strategic intent, but implementation and the containment of risk remain critical problems for most institutions. They have yet to mine the potential value of new products and services by dealing with the costly downside.

CREATING NEW VALUE

Social capital is an extension of human capital based not simply on individual expertise, talent and resources but on the value to be gained by collaborative relationships among colleagues. Client demand for an integrated approach currently outpaces the capacity of banks to deliver from their fragmented structures and competing product lines. Key competitive assets of the future – certain to create new top-line value – are high-quality information and interpretation which develops and delivers innovative solutions for clients. Beyond the current era of the star players, the knowledge edge may create a new generation of bankers fascinated by the potential of working with colleagues to develop outstanding integrated products and services – mining collaborative intelligence and interpretation. This collegiality is already found in commercial banks, where composite deals are more common. In investment banks, collegiality is quickly generated for specific deals, but the relationships and activities are of a temporary nature – lasting until the deal is signed off.

The next generation of senior executives will probably have to know more about strategy, marketing, managing people and controlling complex processes. They will need to generate better understanding of the interface between product specialists and systems people. All these activities will begin to shift investment banking from purely transaction-based business to a form of networked intelligence, servicing and deepening and solidifying client relationships. In such value-added activity, clients, not fellow bankers, may be the biggest source of potential competition. Corporate treasury departments already carry out money market transactions directly. For more complex business, investment bankers will need to become adept at outsmarting treasury people by developing innovative product packages designed to respond to client needs in a much more creative and comprehensive way.

Innovative effort is currently largely confined to product design, which can be easily imitated and commoditized. Future innovative effort might be a package of genuinely integrated products and services which break new ground, extend the parameters of the traditional lines of business – based on customized advisory and intelligence work which cannot be done in a traditional way. Key competitors of the future may be the major accounting firms and management consultants. Full-page ads in the *Financial Times* for institutions as diverse as Warburg Dillon Reed, CSFB and Goldman Sachs already stress 'unrelenting thinking by diverse talent' and 'customized client solutions'. J. P. Morgan's recent campaign personalizes client delivery by stressing the ingenuity and dedication of named employees – 'always willing to go that extra mile'. But how much is still hype?

The banks still retain the edge over the major professional advisory firms, being able to link new intelligence-based products with a customized approach to raising capital through debt, equity, bonds or a variety of channels. Will this edge also be eroded? Wait and see how other potential competitors transform themselves. Many more clients may go to capital markets directly (admittedly currently still a more costly option than using a bank – if a firm does not have a first-rate credit rating) – which enables them to raise long-term funding and retain valued confidentiality.

The real challenge for investment banks is to build a capacity to take advantage of their knowledge edge. This is supremely dependent on getting the right people, gaining their support through effective leadership, and creating a high-performance super-culture over a series of differentiated subcultures. This will be the biggest potential step forward in the first decade of the new century. From the mid-1990s, investment banks began to become clients of business school executive programmes, making a tentative attempt to consider the development of their future leaders.

The sheer complexity of the business, the outstanding potential for marshalling and customizing a wide variety of products offers exciting possibilities for transformation.

'Blue chip' investment banks have always attracted the best and brightest from American MBA programmes, but recently have lost out to new e-business start-ups. They will have to run fast to lure back this entrepreneurial talent. The entry salary and bonus package were not the carrots, as top graduates went to start-up firms for a fraction of the package the banks were offering them. What better time to think seriously about a different career and reward structure? There is a challenging array of opportunities for creating new forms of value in banking which will be able to attract the best people in the years to come – able to replicate the high-risk, high-reward potential that has until recently seen high-flying graduates depart for new arenas. In the UK and Europe, investment banks have not traditionally taken the cream of MBA programmes, which has mostly gone to the large consulting practices.

FROM DOING DEALS TO CLIENT FOCUS

The traditional sources of competitive advantage in investment banking are transaction, information and interpretation. The first two have become commoditized. The latter is the future potential strength. Mining the expert knowledge base of different parts of the organization to integrate sectoral research capability (in, say, utilities, financial services or telecoms with the embedded expertise of products lines such as bonds, equity issues or derivatives) can initiate the process of customization for clients. The current fragmentation of knowledge into separate businesses incurs loss of value because disparate segments of the organization have no consistent means of sharing established expertise or mining integrated innovative potential. Most energy is taken up in the temporary alliances built around specific deals.

Deal-driven networks are transient, discrete and focused. A unique configuration of resources, based on information with a high specific value, is the core of the deal strategy. Deal strategies may have little or no relationship to the overall strategy of the bank, but the potential for lucrative immediate profits will always outweigh longer-term strategic considerations. Deals can be high energy, high reward. Deal teams can create valued temporary collegiality. They initiate the potential for using the same people again in some form – turning strong transient links into longer-term ties among colleagues. But deal teams can be rife with rivalry and conflict, particularly where the shared remuneration for the deal is not clearly spelled out at the outset, or the process of dividing up the spoils becomes itself a source of conflict. Any change in process will make assumed reward unclear and a source of contention. Very often the transient nature of the internal ties which hold the deal together are determined by external links to different segments of the market. This externality is an added pressure to all but the most collegial cultures. Fragmented, competitive organizations tend to be replicated and magnified by the deal environment. It may be simply impossible to build longer-term strong ties among colleagues from rival parts of the business – each with a specific subculture more easily defined by the specific markets they serve than the institutions for which they work. The exit opportunity – push for dissatisfaction; pull for greater gain – perpetually adds extra pressure.

But there are deals and deals – and some undoubtedly introduce valuable initial forms of learning about how other colleagues operate, and the sources of their expertise – however instrumental these are to the specific deal itself. Is it possible to capture and transform the positive energy and expertise of deal teams into a more generalized framework which can become something more than a one-off opportunity? Can the deal networks be transformed and reconfigured into creative networks for client servicing over a longer-term period? Investment banking subcultures might develop into the agile and innovative client-based networks which have become so valued by the best-performing global businesses. Some of the most successful corporations (GE, ABB, Accenture, 3M, Intel) have begun to transform themselves into networked global operations.[2] If investment banks are able to skip the hierarchical stage through which corporates developed, and build new types of networks which will help

	Deal-driven	**Client-focused**
Information	Specific	Interpretive
Structure	Temporary team	Renewable, flexible teams
Management style	Drivers, stars	Collaborators, collegiality
Behaviour	Transient relationships	Sustained relationships
Reward	Deal bonus	Client valuation
		Large salaried input

Figure 11.1 Deal-driven versus client-focused networks.

capture and retain an increasingly larger client base, they will have made a network to network transition which could be of supreme value.

The distinction between deal-driven and client-focused networks may be characterized as in Figure 11.1. There are three significant components required for the transformation from a deal-driven to a client-focused culture: leadership, teamwork and a reform of the current incentive system. Not easy – but the potential gain cannot be ignored and the clear winners will be those institutions which make the effort. Senior banker roles or fast-track solutions have made only a partial impact because they have been grafted onto cultures which have not essentially changed the way they do things. The point of fast track is to circumvent the bureaucracy. Some of the American investment banks, with their drive and energy, have been rather more successful, but this often comes with a tournament culture which can sap energy. Two exceptions might be Goldman Sachs and J. P. Morgan. The Morgan culture was based on relationship banking; its team culture has built strong collegiality and trust which are intrinsic to the business, and it was traditionally focused on lifetime careers. Consensus decision making and allegiance to the core values did have to change in the last decade, as more aggressive major players in the American market seemed to set the leadership pace as well as the tone. Morgan changed the way it did business with greater emphasis on profitability, faster decisions and an abandonment of lifetime commitment. They adapted successfully by extensive consideration and planning of key changes, preserving as much as possible of the old culture. In the new organization, they found it easier to integrate new people from outside the business which added fresh blood.[3]

The basic principles on which Goldman Sachs operate were codified in 1983 when the business began to grow internationally, and it was felt necessary to publish the significant values which executives felt could no longer be transferred informally. These include the usual – client first, teamwork, profit sharing and the key assets of people, capital and reputation.[4] But somehow 'Goldman' seem to give them more sustained meaning than most other organizations (who also use those terms). Since its very successful flotation in 2000, many have watched with interest to see how the Goldman culture will be altered once the pivotal characteristic of partnership is removed. Several partners left prior to listing, reflecting a loss of confidence and trust. Until this time, the firm enjoyed a long history of employee loyalty and a capacity for tolerating even some staggeringly large trading setbacks. 'Goldman's' distinct competitive assets remain its close client relationships, very sophisticated knowledge from the people they recruit with care, and a quite prodigious deal flow. Their initial results in the year of their listing were excellent.

Banks like **ABN AMRO** are successful alternative models for creating and sustaining new forms of added value through integration of different parts of the business. They have every opportunity to exploit the full potential of their network to 78 countries by building collaborative capital internally. They begin with the valuable asset of a very collegial and open culture, and many new recruits attracted from other banks by the potential of excellent capital ratings and global reach. Like other institutions, there is a need to set aside time to encourage colleagues to get together to learn from previous deals (theirs' and competitors'), to promote greater understanding of the wide array of expertise both in corporate and investment banking.

Focusing on the potential for creating more client responsive networks reveals how much effort is needed. The client base in many institutions is very ill-defined and client profitability (even in corporate banking) is often not measured. Understanding the current and potential value of the client is vital to the development of client segmentation. Mapping out activities and respective returns will test the market success of current activities and profile clients for future higher value-based activities and core strengths. To this may be added tests for current product profitability and estimates for the profitability of future innovative products based on integration of expertise.

The traditional matrix of investment banking activities is based on three axes: geography, sector and product. The geographic focus is customarily based on administrative efficiency, but does not necessarily pass the test of whether or not an A-rated client fares equally well in Taipei or Rio. Product segmentation is probably unsustainable, although fragmentation is sustained by the complex nature of these products, which are jealously guarded by their developers. Cross-subsidization of products, which serves internal accounting well, is not in the interests of clients. The move from such traditional areas of convenience to client focus will require fundamental changes in organization as well as remuneration. At present there are very few reward structures for cross-selling – let alone for taking time to develop a more responsive approach to integrated product design and customization. The core strength in product innovation will gradually develop from current segments into more integrated products which will be designed with specific clients more firmly in mind from the outset. With customized research and continual on-line delivery a new and more enduring partnership can be developed with clients wherein the intuitive judgements about product design will be based on client knowledge and perhaps even designed in collaboration with them.

In short, investment bankers need to make more time (and be rewarded for) listening and learning rather than being focused on speed, price and sell. Highly valued interpretation, together with lending and capital fund-raising capacity, will create a win–win situation, enabling those who excel to mine the recurrent value of long-term client relationships.

Building new relationships across the bank, and in collaboration with corporate banking where the institutions are joined in the same group, will add value and make sense. In addition to devising a more satisfactory reward structure for individuals, the assessment of profitability of each segment will have to be altered to take account of more collaborative activity. In the partnership structure of Goldman Sachs, the annual assessment and promotion review was based on a complex – almost arcane – comprehensive review of all activities with colleagues. Significantly it takes subjective assessment into account. They have until now used their partnership culture to avoid a star system. Thus the value of a particular deal is determined according to the contribution of people to the process, meaning that the highest earner may have been a 'sherpa' in a distant location rather than the partner heading the deal. And much more significant than the reward was the review of colleagues which commended this collegial behaviour, earning credit towards eventual partnership. New career structures can be built by different forms of recruitment, development and retention in the investment banks of the future. It may raise the human resource department from its traditionally low status in most organizations.

COLLABORATIVE CAPITAL – A NEW ASSET

The hidden value of a business lies in its intangible assets. Efforts to measure these assets – elusive, subjective or perceptual – are in their infancy. For investment banks (and many other knowledge-based businesses) the embedded value of individual talent and expertise is well established. A newer asset is found in the potential for collaborative capital which over time may build returns that are multiples of the intellectual capital measured as a sum of individual contributions. When this asset is focused on client requirements and develops the capacity to outpace them, it will ensure longer, deeper relationships which themselves can become new sources of capital. Knowing clients very well can help create more highly valued products and recurrent opportunities for building further business. Of highest value of all, perhaps, is trust, when relationships are renewed automatically with little or no effort.

At the end of a decade of growth and globalization of major banking institutions, perhaps the time has come to mine the internal sources of capital which have come together in the decade of agglomeration, but have not yet realized their potential value. These new assets are ballast to the continuing turbulence of market risk; they are a potential insurance policy against further operational risk. Changes in organization, culture, remuneration and the time allocated to creating value from potential collaboration will transform investment banking. The first steps, though, will be the most difficult – to turn the riveted focus of senior management away from short-term results and dealmaking to longer-term transformation and mutual reward.

REFERENCES

1 Endlich, L. (1999) *Goldman Sachs: The Culture of Success*. New York: Little Brown, 17. Although very uncritical of Goldman Sachs, this recent book by a former employee offers valuable information and insight into this important organization.
2 Nohria, N. and S. Ghoshal (1997) *The Differentiated Network: Organizing Multinationals for Value Creation*. San Francisco, CA: Jossey-Bass.
3 Rogers, D. (1993) *The Future of American Banking*. New York: McGraw Hill, 193–255.
4 Endlich, *op. cit*, 88–89.

The Trusted Leader and   12
Releasing the Energy to Succeed

THE TRUSTED LEADER

In this new era of business, a leader is no longer an isolated hero commanding from on high. The leaders who stand out use their interpersonal skills and an emotional appeal to inspire and enthuse people. Leaders are called upon to earn authority without controlling and need to develop trust through openness and excellent communication skills. There are so many books and manuals on the market about leadership that it is easy to get lost in the advice. There is at least some common agreement that successful leaders need vision, energy and strategic direction to earn their authority. Some believe they are set apart by their strong values; others that they are the keeper and interpreter of the strategic vision. A leader helps to develop the collective self-confidence of an organization. Effective leadership can move organizations from current to future states, create visions of potential opportunities and instill employees with commitment to change.[1] Vision is the commodity of leaders, power is their currency and trust, the cohesion that links the leader to the people. 'A leader without trust is like a bird without wings, a pathetic creature able to do little but strut about for a time, weak and vulnerable, accomplishing little and soon displaced.'[2]

Trust is a key ingredient in successful leadership. If leaders practise the art of persuasion[3] they try to engage people in supporting their viewpoint. This can be done so artfully that that people may feel they have freely chosen to agree. Without credibility and trust, this can become manipulation. Trust fosters commitment rather than demanding compliance in the old controlling model of authority. Trust can encourage risk taking, imagination, innovative behaviour and perseverance necessary to a 'knowledge-creating organization',[4] Many of today's knowledge workers are free agents more loyal to their profession and career than to the company. Coaching is an exceptionally useful approach with which a successful leader can deal with people in an entirely new framework. It is a relationship based on mutual trust and understanding.

One of the key supports of successful leadership is a guiding coalition, according to John Kotter. People customarily join a guiding coalition from different organizational functions which may have previously had relationships based on suspicion and low trust. When they are promoted upward there can be a residual lack of trust which means that the formation of the team must be strong enough to overcome parochial games. 'When trust is present, you will usually be able to create teamwork. When it's missing, you won't'.[5] By contrast, the General Electric Corporation – UK (GEC) under Arnold Weinstock in the 1980s was an organization linked only from the centre outwards, with suspicions and mistrust among the different parts of the group. Managers did not speak to each other even within operations like Marconi. Divisions of the company remained separate – avionics and communication, for example – which weakened potential synergies. Weinstock kept senior managers in their own little boxes instead of developing a guiding coalition. They communicated with the centre but not with each other. A former director said 'There was a lack of trust among people. There seemed to be a need to divide and conquer.'[6]

In sharp contrast to GEC, the AES Corporation, a global electricity company, has built a fully empowered workforce. People have power and responsibility throughout the firm for major decisions. Chairman Roger Sant and CEO Dennis Bakke describe their people as 'fully engaged' and 'well-rounded generalists'. The employee-appraisal scheme reflects the basic values of the company: '. . . roughly 50% of a person's compensation is based on technical factors such as financial performance, safety and environmental impact. The other 50% is based on how well people individually and as a group understand and adhere to the four shared values –

fairness, integrity, social responsibility and fun.'[7] How does real empowerment such as this redefine the role of the leader? In AES, leaders have four roles: advisor, guardian of the principles, accountability office and chief encourager.[8]

The most successful leaders may use a combination of leadership styles depending on the circumstances. There are four leadership styles which affect climate positively, according to recent research. These are the authoritative style which mobilizes people towards the vision; the affiliative style which creates harmony and builds emotional bonds; the democratic style which forges consensus through participation and the coaching style which develops people.[9] Emotional intelligence can be very useful to a leader who can become a source of energy in an organization. Based on self-awareness and self-management together with social awareness and social skill, some of its essential characteristics include trustworthiness, empathy and building bonds.[10] Goleman's work on emotional intelligence develops the characteristics of trustworthiness as acting ethically, building trust through reliability and authenticity, admitting mistakes and confronting unethical actions.[11]

Southwest Airlines is another example of a firm where empowerment actually means something in practice. And they are one of the top performers in the industry, operating a short-haul low-cost service. A leader in Southwest is an enabler. CEO Herb Kelleher described it as turning the organizational pyramid upside down. 'At the bottom you've got the people in headquarters. Up there at the top you've got the people who are out there in the field, on the front line. They're the ones who are making things happen, not us. The people out there are the experts. [At head office] we're the supply corps, we're not the heroes. We supply the heroes. The heroes are out there.'[12]

In contrast, Bob Crandall, the chairman of American Airlines, chose a confrontational route in dealing with staff in 1997: 'The impasse at American was about trust. When it is lacking in your company, it can cost you deeply — as American's bean counters are currently learning all too well. It's still a bit surprising that Crandall has allowed employee trust to deteriorate so badly and with such dire consequences.' 'Employees are units of expense to him, not assets,' said Captain Jeff Jones, a spokesman for the pilots' union. 'Money is everything and people cost him money. Pilots don't trust him. ...'[13] The seeds of mistrust were a two-tier wage scale for pilots, belittling them to analysts, and a threatened shutdown unless they agreed to concessions. Crandall's combative personality became the focus of labour talks. These things tarnished the excellent achievements which Crandall made in technology, development of the Sabre ticketing system and being the first to promote customer loyalty through a frequent-flier programme. Crandall at American makes a study in contrast with Kelleher at Southwest, where pilots signed up for ten-year contracts and chipped in to get him a custom-built Harley-Davidson in the airline's colours.

All leaders face the challenge of overcoming resistance to change. Trust is achieved through positioning, according to Warren Bennis and Bert Nanus. Positioning is for them a set of actions necessary to implement the vision. 'Positioning aims at building a new community of common interests, shared circumstances and mutual trust. ... The leader is responsible for the set of ethics and norms that govern the behaviour of people in an organization.'[14]

Trust is the emotional glue that binds the leader to his or her people. An accumulation of trust helps to foster the legitimacy of leadership which can be earned. It helps as the leader resolves crucial dilemmas and reformulates the vision, so essential to the rapid changes in today's business world. 'Successful leaders are driven by high ambition, maintain a certain sense of humility and undertake a constant search for trust.'[15] This sense of humility has been widely explored and relates to empathy and selectively showing weakness. It builds solidarity with followers. The new leader no longer displays the old comrade behaviour of being 'one of the boys', often heard in respect of great loyalty to 'my people'. The new relationship is more than one based on loyalty and paternalism. By selectively showing weakness, a leader 'can expose vulnerability and reveal his approachability and humanity'.[16]

There are two major facets to leadership: task/practical management and relationship/emotional approach. Increasingly feedback assessments for managers will focus on the effectiveness of managing relationships in contrast to managing output. Career managers in the future will be selected for their managerial competencies rather than their technical expertise.[17] One of the key management paradoxes is the tension between the need for sophisticated expertise and the necessity for broad-based communication skills and plain talking. Arnold Weinstock rejected this paradox entirely. In a television interview, he said, 'You have to distinguish between your responsibility as a manager and your personal feelings. A manager has the responsibility to make the best use of resources which are entrusted to his care, and that doesn't include people.'[18] His combative style bred excessive caution and defensiveness among many. Senior managers were reluctant to stick their necks out with a new idea which might have made a great deal of money for the Group. It discouraged innovation.

Leadership has an emotional appeal which encourages people to reveal their differences and capitalize on what is unique about them. In appealing for trust, the leader demonstrates self trust and encourages an environment in which others may feel comfortable to follow his lead. But how it is achieved has to be highly personal; the recipe books just do not work. There is no universal formula. The many biographies of successful business leaders, and the formula books, cannot cover the unique situation in which the leader finds him or herself.

Informal networks are particularly valuable for handling the unexpected problems which have grown in importance in the recent business environment. A measure of leadership effectiveness could easily be built on the capacity to maintain extensive informal networks within and outside the firm – in government, politics, the media and the business community.

All organizations depend on shared meanings and interpretations of reality, which facilitate coordinated action. Leadership in the world's most admired companies focuses and delivers on key values. They are organizations in which people feel that they are treated fairly. 'Trust is a critical part of that equation. There is a strong relationship between the effectiveness of a leader and the extent to which people trust him or her. With trust comes candour and the willingness of people to speak their minds.'[19] With the security of trust, people are willing to take risks for the leader and the company. Leaders who seek to get the best from their people are instrumental in creating an environment in which they can give their best. They can encourage a sense of belonging which is based on more than loyalty. Leaders who can create such an environment do not need to practise persuasion, as the potential alignment of a leader and his people comes naturally. People follow without persuasion.

Some advice to business leaders is diluted in a din of hype. Perhaps there is now room for a more thoughtful approach. Contemplation about how to build trust will lead a quiet and thoughtful manager to trust his people rather than flout his policy of empowerment. Leaders who espouse trust will strengthen the bonds between people. 'Quiet management is about the infusion of change that seeps steadily and profoundly, rather than having it thrust upon people in superficial episodes. ... Quiet management is about thoughtfulness rooted in experience. Words like wisdom, trust, dedication and judgement apply.'[20]

As guardian of the vision, the successful leader is a storykeeper and storyteller. An essential factor of leadership is the capacity to influence and give meaning to members of the organization. A leader achieves his effectiveness through the stories he relates. The innovative leader knows where his people are coming from and where they will go. He may find a story that is latent among his people.[21] A model for this is clearly someone like Gandhi or Churchill, but it can apply to businesses as well, since the strategic vision encourages identification or alignment built on the best that people have to offer. A business leader needs to keep the story simple, but it is helpful to use metaphors, analogies and examples. It is then reinforced through leading by example and walking the talk. If the vision is believable, and helps to create self trust among people, they will easily give their best. An innovative leader brings new attention or a fresh twist to the story. The story needs to make sense to the people. A visionary leader creates a new story and persuades the people to make it their own: when the business must change tack because of competitive pressures, a trusted leader can easily bring his people with him. Trust will have been built on openness and communication throughout the changes. As the leader resolves crucial dilemmas, he brings his people with him. The story is more than a theme or a message – it is a dynamic interaction between leader and follower. Among the most powerful stories are those that deal with identity and have their roots in personal experience. They are among the most significant and lasting.[22] This is why the qualities recommended for business leadership include revealing oneself to the people and capitalizing on uniqueness.

A story can help to create trust because it links the people in a common cause for which the story creates meaning. Sometimes the audience is different. A business leader has three principal audiences; colleagues and employees, shareholders, and the public. With colleagues and employees, the story helps to promote the confidence that they can rely on one another to do their best. This collegiality begins at board level, where the harmony between the chairman and the chief executive is the pivotal relationship. Personality clashes are so damaging. An exceptional leader will surround himself with a talented and complementary team. No successful company can long sustain constant boardroom battles which leak out to the press and raise shudders in the markets. In the marketplace the leader needs to make strategic moves credible. These are customarily based on shareholder value which in turn is often based on the quality of management in an organization. Some of the best-performing companies and the most long lasting ones had policies which put their people first. Dealing with the public is not always a matter of persuasion (or manipulation) by the public affairs department. Companies with a good reputation become known.

Trust implies fairness and openness to all stakeholders. This is related to tolerance and dependability and is exercised through openness and communication of mutual respect. Successful leaders have learned the great value of consistency when dealing with different constituencies. When all these are in place, a leader can begin to build a reputation which is renewable with little effort. All these factors leave ample scope for personal adaptation and the development of a personal signature in the process of building trust. Trust can increase the leader's scope for action. Among the most admired companies there is a perception that people are treated fairly: trust is a critical part of the equation.

Trust is the basis from which the scope for action is enlarged beyond the ordinary. It has versatility and resilience. As the penalty area of social action recedes, more can be accomplished on the basis of common understanding. The need for rules, controls and surveillance contracts in the face of common values and assumptions from which energy can begin to flow. Low trust can undermine the most innovative and robust strategy. It reduces the scope for action, relying on self-serving behaviour, politics and a tournament culture. The blind spots of leadership arise when the following factors are apparent:

- Blind ambition
- Unrealistic goals
- Relentless striving
- Driving others too hard
- Power-hungry
- Insatiable need for recognition
- Preoccupation with appearances
- Need to seem perfect.[23]

Economic and social changes have generated new demands for management by consent rather than coercion, based on new employee expectations about work, authority and responsibility. People today are looking for more than a low trust organization as a place to work, as our case studies have demonstrated. Employees who do a good job want to be recognized for their contribution to the outcome. Organizations which stress participation indicate that high trust is important to building and sustaining employee commitment. Involving people on the basis of trust offers the opportunity of taking the working relationship beyond the simple contractual basis of work. It can make a new contribution to the quality of working life, which may be both more meaningful and satisfying for employees, and more profitable for the firm.

Trust creates a climate in which learning and innovation have an opportunity to develop and renew themselves on a continual basis. By providing a resilient form of glue which can hold together vital forces within the company, trust releases the energy to accomplish a wider scope of activities. Trust relies on a clear purpose, structure and boundaries which release energy into the field of social action in the firm. Clarity and workable boundaries are essential. Confusion and lack of clarity are trust's natural enemies.

TRUST: RELEASING ENERGY

Trust is enhanced by reputation. Maintaining it is the real test. Successful companies can be judged on their recruitment and retention. They offer a place to work that engages people's talents and efforts. For senior people the firm may invest in their employability as managers or specialists rather than assuming that they will stay forever with the firm. This new moral contract is based on an open book of assumptions on the part of employee and employer. It relies on clarity and transparency and assumes respective responsibility for employability from both employee and employer. All these components ensure a new form of trust which is far removed from job security.

Trust can release energy in people and enlarge the scope of human and intellectual capital in the firm, by encouraging people to give more of themselves and build commitment to strategic goals. The investment cost in trust is not high. The maintenance cost is low. Trust can be a key lever in increasing productivity and quality by encouraging consultation, listening to what people have to say. If people are reluctant managers or unwilling to accept new responsibility, a serious look at the trust component in the culture of the organization is essential.

There are ten major factors which together demonstrate how leaders can promote trust:

- Communicate the vision and thereby capture people's imagination and support
- Offer a constant flow of information about strategic direction in a form which can make an impact
- Be consistent, making it obvious when radical changes must take place

- Demonstrate competence to your peers and self-assurance to all others
- Be reliable so people can count on you
- Be open with people: walk the talk or use e-mails
- Coach rather than direct, seeking people's own resourcefulness to rectify errors
- Practise fairness and set an example for others
- Demonstrate respect and recognition for efforts which people make
- Show care and concern.

Gary Hamel's strategic consulting firm, Strategos, operates on the principle of getting people out of their comfort zone, as he and his colleagues find that people are jaded on initiatives and are deeply sceptical. The process they encourage is to engage people by taking them to Silicon Valley to experience the innovation process. The group they work with develops rapport, solidarity and trust, and become the advance team of change in the organization. Time is set aside to encourage entrepreneurial behaviour. From this core group new ideas are developed, which may even seem 'off the wall' initially, but if developed and refined could prove the contribution to ensure a breakthrough which can generate new wealth creation. From apathy, the energy and excitement grows with the process, and forms a new basis for trust.

The release of individual or collaborative creativity, and the encouragement of innovation, rely on an environment of trust (Figure 12.1). Distrust is the enemy of this process, since people do not wish to invest

People can do more things

They do them more effectively

They give more of themselves

They have been waiting for an opportunity to do so

Figure 12.1 Trust releases energy.

themselves fully. They do not create significant relationships with others that can yield more than the sum of individual contributions.

While the lessons about the management of people have become recognized, there is still a long way to go to reap the benefits. The contribution which trust can make is to introduce a new set of ideas on the value of relationships. There is still a strong preference among senior managers for the drive to control, rather then divest authority. This may be a result of their own lack of self trust or self-confidence. The factors which make the management of people a success are complicated, take time, cannot be based on advice purchased from the outside, have to be done within.

- Consider the experience of working together with an individual or group of people when the relationship works and creates a buzz. Trust may account for the added value that makes the situation seem to hum. Will the positive atmosphere and excitement continue to be sustained by trust?
- It is easier to change direction rapidly when people share a common understanding and are pleased to support the new initiative, making it their own. Is the acceptance of the new initiative based on trust?
- The rapid and free exchange of ideas on a new problem or a client account can generate innovative solutions. What does trust contribute to innovation?
- A team may find the scope to go into issues that may have eluded others and offer a novel approach to solving a long-standing problem. Is trust a component of this success?
- Working together on the same wavelength in circumstances of mutual respect has social value which can build. How does trust contribute to social capital?

Why is there new attention to motivating and stimulating people? Why has new significance been given to otherwise well-known reflections? Simply, it is the squeeze on margins, and the intensity of competition, that has revalued the contribution that people can make to competitive success. That contribution is best released by creating and

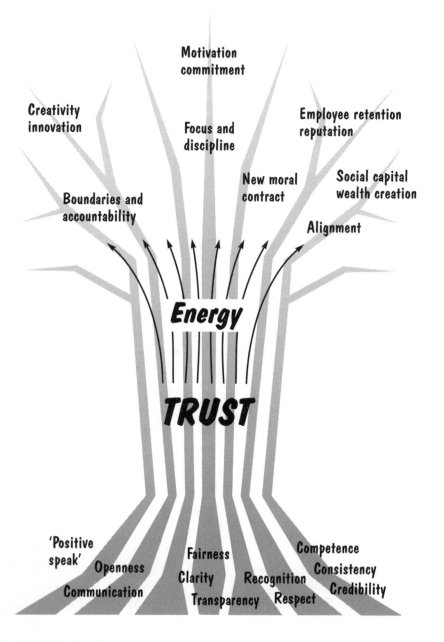

Figure 12.2 The trust tree.

sustaining trust in the organization, by making it part of the strategy and systems.

THE TRUST TREE

Figure 12.2 is an analogy of the energy and value creation implied in the seasonal growth of a living tree. The roots provide the stability and take in the food and other nourishment for the growth of the trust tree. The key branches yield the flowering of growth which depict the outcomes and benefits of trust.

A strong tree with solid, well-established roots and vibrant seasonal growth will be able to resist minor disturbances such as floods and drought (like market challenges, technology breakthroughs). It contains within it the elements of resistance and renewal. A tree may not survive a bolt of lightning or an earthquake (a major competitive challenge from a company like Enron, Intel or Microsoft, which can alter the stakes entirely). It may be severely damaged as far back as the roots, but it may grow again over a long period of time (rebuilding from the base), perhaps always stunted compared to its original capacity and in a different shape from its former one.

Shareholder value is created when the branches flourish and grow strong, relying less and less on the continued inputs of nutrients, as in the formative period of growth. The cost of maintenance of each tree can reduce over time.

Forest management of a group of trees, like group shareholder value, relies on an assessment of the resilience of assets. Thinning and felling are always necessary in order to maintain the value of assets and stimulate growth. Forest management assesses the overall yield. Shareholder value is created by the felling of trees which need replacement.

TRUST: RELEASING VALUE

Trust can reduce the cost of doing business with all stakeholders by simply reducing the cost of building and developing successful working relationships. This can be seen as a reduction in the cost of transacting business.

Reducing the transaction costs saves time, which translates into earnings. An employee who understands his or her role in contributing to corporate goals, and is willing to contribute fully, has a low transaction cost. Politics, backbiting and poor working relationships contribute to high transaction costs. A major insurance company, which has a full (even over-full) agenda of demutualization, international acquisition and transformation to a financial service business, felt the undertow on its ambitions very rapidly. Its business unit heads (newly charged with P&L responsibility) refused to cooperate with each other to create a group services strategy; new initiatives were regarded with the utmost scepticism and killed; much time was taken up in office politics and hiding real results to avoid blame. This was all happening at a time when they needed to make themselves more transparent for public scrutiny as a public company. The eventual impact on their capacity to act became obvious; it will inevitably impact on the share price before too long.

The individual bonus systems of investment banks are quintessential transaction-based institutions. Goldman Sachs under its partnership system has built one of the most successful and profitable integrated global banking positions by giving higher rewards to 'sherpas' and intermediates rather than the person or team that signed off the deal. With a complex reward system based on helping other colleagues to complete a deal, the development of a deal is rewarded more highly than completion. In the ruthlessly individualistic and materialistic world of global finance, the high value of networking and building colleague relationships to make a successful deal has become a leading culture in the business. Difficult to emulate, the Goldman Sachs partnership structure has its imitators. But the culture is crucial. New international deal-making is based on extensive networking across products, functions and countries. Effective client servicing in the future will be based no longer on individual high-flyer performance alone, but on specialist expertise the world over.

The strategic shift which trust and social capital offer is the movement from appropriating value in the organization to providing an atmosphere which supports and sustains value creation. In a trusting environment people contribute fully and create value though their knowledge, skill motivation and ingenuity. Such value creation has become the recommended strategic path for successful future competition. Becoming an industry leader by altering the playing field and changing the rules of the game initiates wealth creation. Successfully creating wealth cannot only be based on the most innovative ideas of a chief executive or a top team. It relies on changing the way the organization thinks and operates. Ken Leigh may be credited with the dramatic shift in electricity production in shaping the US corporation, Enron, but it is Enron's innovative corporate culture and capacity to take advantage of specific opportunities which make its performance outstanding.

Trust needs to be built into the strategy and systems of a company if the mobilization and maximization of resources is to be gained. It cannot be an afterthought. It is not the responsibility of the HR department. Too often strategic ideas fall by the wayside because of a failure to understand the key intermediary processes, like trust creation, which contribute to success. Either it becomes part of the way things are done, from the chief executive throughout the organization, or it fails.

Trust is a calculable asset, but as yet those of us who write about it have only begun to develop measures which allow people to estimate their score on high or low trust. These are relatively rudimentary. Even without reliable measures, though, we must continue to address the hard questions about the calculable contribution of trust and the cost of building trust as opposed to counting the cost of low trust. Taking a look at the much-used website of 'The 100 Best Companies to Work for in America', there is a close link between morale and performance. 'Of the

---

TRUST REDUCES OPPORTUNISM

It significantly reduces the cost of doing business

Trust creates new scope and value

Value creation is critical to competitive success

Figure 12.3 Trust and competitive success.

61 firms that have been publicly traded (1993–98), 45 yielded higher returns to shareholders than an index of all large and small companies. The 61 companies averaged annual returns of 27.5% vs. 17.3% for the overall average.... A recent Gallup Survey of 55 000 American workers attempted to match employee attitudes with company results. The four attitude findings which correlate strongly with higher profits are: workers feel they are given an opportunity to do what they do best; they believe their opinions count; they sense that their fellow workers are committed to quality; and they've made a direct connection between their work and the company's mission'.[24]

Shareholder value focuses on results and goals. It seems to be diametrically opposed to the new paradigm of the creation of social capital through trust and its contribution to competitive advantage. But must this be so? Those supporting a deeper sense of strategic purpose in business talk of wealth creation and breaking the current mould of competition.

The movement of the share price represents a company's market value. But are horizons so short that they can ignore compelling evidence that companies which are often spectacularly profitable face collapse? Delivering maximum return to investors must be balanced by the interests of other constituents, particularly customers and employees. It is false to consider that if shareholders win they must do so at the expense of employees. In the best-performing companies the reverse is true and employees have benefited along with shareholders in the value created – having been instrumental in creating that value.

There is considerable interest in long-term transformation and its contribution to shareholder value. Companies which last and demonstrate profitable returns are often those which focus on the valued contribution of their people. We may see a convergence of the paradigms of long-term transformation and of shareholder value. The value of trust may be a core component in this potential convergence. Trust offers resilience in our turbulent business environment. It can create value. It releases the energy to succeed.

REFERENCES

1 Bennis, W. and B. Nanus (1997) *Leaders: Strategies for Taking Charge*. New York: HarperBusiness, 17.

2 Nanus, B. (1989) *The Leader's Edge*. Chicago and New York: Contemporary Books.

3 Conger, J. (1998) *Winning 'em Over: A New Model for Managing in the Age of Persuasion*. New York: Simon and Schuster.

4 Senge, P. (1997) 'Communities of Leaders and Learners'. *Harvard Business Review* September-October, 32.

5 Kotter, J.P. (1996) *Leading Change*. Boston, MA: Harvard Business School Press, 61–62.

6 Brummer, A. and R. Cowe, (1997) *Weinstock*. New York: HarperBusiness, 308.

7 Wetlaufer, S. (1999) 'Organizing for Empowerment: An Interview with AES's Roger Sant and Dennis Bakke'. *Harvard Business Review* January–February, 116.

8 Wetlaufer, S. *op. cit.*, 119–20.

9 The authoritative style has the strongest statistical relationship to climate. Research done by Hay McBer using a random sample of nearly 4000 executives. Cited in Goleman, D. (2000) 'Leadership that gets Results'. *Harvard Business Review* March–April, 82–3.

10 Goleman, D. (1998) *Working with Emotional Intelligence*, London: Bloomsbury, 26–7.

11 Goleman, D. *op cit.*, 89.

12 PaikSunoo, B. (1995) 'How Fun Flies at Southwest Airlines'. *Personnel Journal* June, 66.

13 Lieber, R.B. (1997) 'Bon Crandall's Boo Boos'. *Fortune* 28 April.

14 Bennis and Nanus, *op cit.*, 172–3.

15 Champney, J. and N. Nohria, (1996) *Fast Forward*. Cambridge, MA: Harvard Business School Press.

16 Goffee, R. and G. Jones (2000) 'Why Should Anyone be Led by You?' *Harvard Business Review* September–October, 64.

17 Goffee, R. and J. Hunt (1998) 'The End of Management? Classroom versus Boardroom'. *Financial Times Mastering Management* 20 March.

18 Brummer and Cowe, *op cit.*, 134.

19 Kets deVries, M. (2000) 'Beyond Sloan: Trust is at the Core of Corporate Values'. *Financial Times Mastering Management* 2 October.

20 Minzberg, H. (1998) 'Softly, Softly over Blood and Thunder'. *Financial Times*, 13 October.

21 Gardiner, H. (1995) *Leading Minds: An Anatomy of Leadership*. New York: HarperCollins, 305–6.

22 *Ibid.*

23 Kaplan, R.E. (1998) 'Beyond Ambition'. Cited in Goleman, *op. cit.*, 65–66.

24 Grant, L. (1998) 'You Inc: the 100 Best Companies to Work for in America/ Happy Workers, High Returns'. *Fortune* 12 January.

Index